1

More Advance Praise for *UNMASKED*

"Every conservative must read *Unmasked*—a crucial tool to counter the left in the ongoing battle to save our country and restore freedom in America."
—**DAVID MCINTOSH**
PRESIDENT OF THE CLUB FOR GROWTH

"Bozell and his staff of media watchers compile quotes, outrages, and studies that devastate the idea that the news media are referees of our political debates. It's even worse than you think. *Unmasked* will prove it."
—**FORMER SENATOR JIM DEMINT**
CHAIRMAN, CONSERVATIVE PARTNERSHIP INSTITUTE

"Brent Bozell has been exposing the media's shameless liberal bias for more than thirty years. But it's never been worse out there than it is under President Trump. Bozell shows how the 'objective' press has crossed every line, erased every boundary, and avoided every ounce of decency in going after this president."
—**ADAM BRANDON**
PRESIDENT OF FREEDOMWORKS

"*Unmasked* is a vitally important and timely book that exposes the massive propaganda attack designed to undermine and even topple a duly elected president and his administration."

—**EDWIN MEESE**
FORMER ATTORNEY GENERAL
UNDER RONALD REAGAN

"Brent Bozell and Tim Graham document the war on the President—the media's abandonment of even a pretext of impartiality—in a must read for every American."

—**RON ROBINSON**
PRESIDENT OF YOUNG AMERICA'S
FOUNDATION

"*Unmasked* is a carefully documented analysis of how the media, and their Hollywood allies, have been at war against Donald Trump from the get-go. What has sent them over the edge, as the authors make plain, is their utter failure to convince the public that they're right. Bozell and Graham have hit this one out of the park, dazzling the reader with indisputable evidence."

—**BILL DONOHUE**
PRESIDENT OF CATHOLIC LEAGUE
FOR RELIGIOUS AND CIVIL RIGHTS

"Brent Bozell alerts and enlightens us on the agenda of an ideological liberal progressive media machine. Benjamin Franklin challenged us, 'a Republic if you can keep it.' Bozell's book enables us to meet that challenge to preserve the last great hope for mankind, these United States of America."

—LIEUTENANT COLONEL ALLEN B. WEST
(US ARMY, RETIRED), MEMBER,
112TH US CONGRESS

"Fake news is real! Brent Bozell and Tim Graham unmask the news media, clearly revealing that they have become the opposition party to constitutional governance."

—TONY PERKINS
PRESIDENT, FAMILY RESEARCH
CENTER AND PRESIDENT, COUNCIL
FOR NATIONAL POLICY

"The 'objective' press is constantly tilting the field of politics, engaging in all kinds of unsportsmanlike conduct. What makes *Unmasked* so devastating is that the evidence it provides is irrefutable. Conservatives must read this book."

—SENATOR MIKE LEE
R-UTAH

UNMASKED

UNMASKED

Big Media's War Against Trump

L. BRENT BOZELL III
AND TIM GRAHAM

Humanix Books
www.humanixbooks.com

Humanix Books

UNMASKED
Copyright © 2019 by Humanix Books
All rights reserved

Humanix Books, P.O. Box 20989, West Palm Beach, FL 33416, USA
www.humanixbooks.com | info@humanixbooks.com

Humanix Books is a division of Humanix Publishing, LLC. Its trademark, consisting of the word "Humanix," is registered in the Patent and Trademark Office and in other countries.

ISBN: 978-163006-115-9 (Hardcover)
ISBN: 978-163006-116-6 (E-book)

Printed in the United States of America
10 9 8 7 6 5 4 3 2 1

For Rush Limbaugh, an old friend.

One shudders to consider where
the country would be today but for you.

Contents

Preface

"I Was Prepared Not to Like Donald Trump"

HE HAD THAT CELEBRITY handle, "The Donald," but for most people he was just Trump, and I confess that I never cared much for Trump. Blowhard, raunchy playboy, controversial businessman, endless self-promoter, jerk—all these things defined the public Donald Trump as seen by his critics. Politics never seemed to be a top-shelf concern for this man, but when he did speak out, the narrative was doctrinaire liberal Democrat, championing Obama, Bill Clinton, and Hillary Clinton while celebrating Planned Parenthood, single-payer health insurance, environmental excesses, and the like.

In recent years he'd been singing from a different sheet. He was becoming increasingly critical of President Obama, but it came with an inexplicable fixation on that damn birth certificate, which all along was the least provable and therefore most irrelevant accusation against the President. It was little more than a clarion call for conspiracy theorists and certainly unbecoming of a dignified contender.

Trump had made noises about running in 2008, but virtually nobody took him seriously, and when nothing materialized, those who bothered to care chalked it up to another Trump publicity stunt. Again in 2012 he flirted with a presidential run. "I maintain the strong conviction that if I were to run, I would be able to win the primary and ultimately, the general election," he boasted. But again nothing. Bluster? Fear? The realization that he couldn't win? No telling. Trump was Trump.

But in 2014 and early 2015, things seemed to be changing. He was becoming more comprehensively outspoken in his condemnation of Obama and the Democrats, and though he didn't seem to be wildly enthusiastic about the GOP, it was becoming evident that that was his destination. Word circulated that he was hiring staff in the early-primary states. More telling than this, Trump was doing deliberate outreach to some of the strongest voices in the conservative movement, such as my old friend talk radio giant Mark Levin, along with some of the most influential activist leaders in the movement, such as Citizens United head David Bossie, a longtime companion in the political trenches.

It was Bossie who urged me to meet Donald Trump. I was skeptical. When I questioned Trump's sudden conversion to the side of the angels, Bossie was quick to defend it: "He's the real deal." When I questioned his seriousness of purpose, Bossie was equally enthusiastic. "I think this time he's gonna do it!"

On December 5, 2014, I received an e-mail from then-Trump aide Sam Nunberg inviting me to meet Mr. Trump in New York. I accepted.

On February 26, I arrived at Trump Tower. Walking into the lobby of the twenty-sixth floor, I was struck by how dark it seemed. Staffers were coming and going, busily but quietly. There seemed to be something surreal about the place. We were ushered into "Mr. Trump's" office. Everyone but everyone called him "Mr. Trump" or "sir." I expected a vast gilded throne room akin to those pictures of his gaudy penthouse. To be sure it was polished, with a magnificent view of the Manhattan landscape, but it lacked the aura of a business tycoon, especially one who designs and constructs his own skyscrapers. The desk wasn't even centered in the room; instead it was pressed against a wall. He sat behind that desk looking like just another corporate senior staff, not the Man Himself.

He came to life instantly. After introductions, we began to chat, but almost immediately a staffer, member interrupted. He approached the desk and handed "Mr. Trump" a report, maybe twenty or twenty-five pages long. Taking possession of it, Trump placed it on his desk and explained that this was his new bio. "It's very, very good!" he enthused as he urged me to read it (though he never gave me a copy). There it was, Braggadocio Trump. He stood and gave us the tour of the trophies along his wall: Mike Tyson's heavyweight championship belt, Tom Brady's Super Bowl helmet, one of Shaquille O'Neal's sneakers, and a framed photo of him shaking President Reagan's hand, to name some of them. Each was a "good friend" of his, and as he recounted how each item came into his possession, you sensed you were being treated to the VIP tour every visitor entering that office received. But I was not turned off. There was something endearing here. It was clear that Trump thoroughly enjoyed being *the Donald*.

Off we went to lunch and to the next surprise. I expected that we'd dine in a private room or perhaps the private room in a swanky restaurant not just because of his pomposity but because of the vicissitudes of celebrity. No such thing. We took the elevator down to the now famous escalator to the Trump Grill. Tourists milling about all recognized him and called out his name. He waved simple hellos and smiled. He made it a point to stop and greet some of the staff, especially the waiters and vendors selling memorabilia at the kiosks. We took a table, ordered, and began to talk.

And for the next forty-five minutes I visited with someone else.

I've never spent almost an hour in conversation with a man who was the exact opposite of everything I knew—or thought I knew—him to be. Bombastic, yes, but now he didn't come across as a braggart. He was proud of his successes, but now he was not boastful. He talked a lot, but by no means did he corner the conversation. He spoke in a low voice and earnestly. He asked questions and listened intently. He was razor-sharp, focused on his guest's answers, prodding and probing, nodding quietly when in agreement, and when at odds he pushed back softly, gently—two words I would have thought could never appear in a sentence also containing the word "Trump." His intelligence was clearly evident. But so was there a thoroughly unexpected—dare I say it?—humility and graciousness.

He wanted to know: Did I think he should run? It was clear to me that he'd already made up his mind and it would take something extraordinary to dissuade him. He'd been told I was supporting Ted Cruz, but I reminded him of this immediately so that there would be no misunderstanding.

My answer was no and yes. I wasn't going to lie. I was convinced he couldn't win, and I owed it to my host to tell him so. But I urged him to run nonetheless. One, he needed to scratch the itch, and with all his scratch he might actually enjoy it. Two, in American politics it sometimes takes more than one attempt to reach the summit, especially when there is dirty laundry to be washed in the court of public opinion, and God knows he had plenty of that. But those were minor points. There was a much more compelling reason.

It's my belief that no politician can control our runaway federal government, as large as it is inept—never mind reduce it. I reminded this businessman of the Grace Commission, launched by President Ronald Reagan in 1982 and chaired by the industrialist Peter Grace. His mandate was to use his business expertise to cut the size of the federal government as a means toward the end of reducing the power centralized in Washington.

I wanted Cruz to win, but wouldn't it be terrific if he then tapped Donald Trump to form the Trump Commission to make sense of the federal mess? Wouldn't it be music to America's ears to hear "You're fired!" several hundred thousand times to rid us of that obnoxious, arrogant, and criminally incoherent creature known as the federal bureaucrat? This, I told my host, was my dream, and it might happen if businessman Trump focused his campaign on this message.

Trump listened intently but was not convinced. "I think I can win. I really do." He said this several times, but with no chest-thumping. He said it quietly, thoughtfully. "I really do think I can win."

We chatted more about the upcoming race, and then it was time to wrap things up. Trump asked me if he'd supported the Media Research Center (MRC), which he praised strongly. I told him he hadn't, and he advised that this would change. We walked back toward the elevators for a good-bye, but not before stopping at the gift stand, where he grabbed a handful of Trump ties, Trump cuff links, and Trump cologne, dutifully celebrating the merits of each item before bequeathing them to his guests.

(Sure enough, a week later a check for $5,000 from the Trump Foundation arrived with Trump's handwritten emphasis, "In honor of the Great Brent!")

Trump was about the most charismatic man I ever met.

Charismatic can mean different things, of course. St. John Paul II had a charisma that left a worldwide television audience hearing the roars of *Santo Súbito!* coming from tens of thousands attending his funeral. On the other hand, Vlad the Impaler probably exuded a certain charisma of his own as he ordered fields filled with thousands of Turkish prisoners shish-kebabbed into the soil. In Trump's case, however, I had never expected to find the word associated with him in any capacity. I left lunch still believing he couldn't win but now wondering just how far he might go if America got to know this Trump.

Three and a half months later Trump announced his candidacy in the same lobby, and the Greatest Show on Earth 2016 was under way. The man I met was nowhere to be found now that he was on stage. From start to finish Trump embraced the persona of the bad boy of politics, breaking all the rules of presidential campaign discourse, showing a striking inability to deliver a speech or, worse, as some stressed derisively, to deliver a complete sentence. There wasn't a hint of humility, or gentility, or thoughtfulness, or kindness—all the things he'd shown me. Immediately he shot to the head of the class, so Team Trump was happy.

I didn't like the way he was doing it, and he wasn't convincing many of us that he was a conservative.

I had endorsed Cruz because I've never questioned his conservative bona fides on anything. I can count on one hand the members of Congress about whom I'd say this. I've grown weary of betrayals coming from faux conservatives who cynically wrap themselves around a movement they don't support in order to get elected, and then reelected.

The GOP leadership is even more cynical.

In electing Obama in 2008, the American people had emphatically not endorsed the radical left-wing agenda that would follow. Within just two years the American people wanted the Democrats thrown out of the House, especially after the passage of Obamacare. The Tea Party was born and political insurrection was in the air. John Boehner read those tea leaves correctly, embraced the revolution, and rode it to victory in 2010.

But the Tea Party had not embraced Boehner. This was in no way an endorsement of a party that had betrayed conservatives time and again.

Did Boehner fundamentally understand this? Did he understand the GOP still needed to restore the trust of its conservative base? In a private meeting on the eve of the election I asked him that question. The look on his face betrayed his supreme displeasure. "Yes," he conceded angrily through gritted teeth, and then abruptly turned away.

"Yes" became "Screw you" the moment he assumed the mantle of Speaker in January of 2011, beginning with the refusal to honor his pledge to defund Obamacare, which could have been accomplished with his very first spending bill. It wasn't just Obamacare. Boehner refused to challenge Obama on anything of consequence. It is incorrect to blame just Obama for the crazy spending sprees that gave us the greatest expansion of federal power and taxpayer debt in history. The Boehner-led House went along, every step of the way.

In 2014, then Senate Minority Leader McConnell traveled from one campaign event to the next, roaring his pledge to repeal Obamacare "root and branch." It was that pledge to America that led to the GOP's stunning capture of the US Senate in November. Just one month later Republican liberals and Democratic liberals joined Majority Leader–elect McConnell in voting to write yet another check, this one for an entire year, funding all of the Obama's priorities, including 100 percent of Obamacare. It was yet another betrayal from a GOP leadership that long ago abandoned its conservative principles, root and branch.

Now Donald Trump, a lifelong Democrat supporting one liberal position after another while funding and championing leftist politicians such as Bill and Hillary Clinton, was telling America he was a conservative Republican. Call me jaded, but I wasn't buying it.

The more I heard him embrace a conservative agenda, the more I feared that this was nothing more than cynical manipulation, and I said so publicly. When *National Review* publisher Jack Fowler asked me to pen a statement that would reflect that sentiment for an upcoming issue of *NR* devoted in its entirety to a corporate denunciation of the Donald, I agreed to do so.

> A real conservative walks with us. Ronald Reagan read *National Review* and *Human Events* for intellectual sustenance; spoke annually to the Conservative Political Action Conference, Young Americans for Freedom, and other organizations to rally the troops; supported Barry Goldwater when the GOP mainstream turned its back on him; raised money for countless conservative groups; wrote hundreds of op-eds; and delivered even more speeches, everywhere championing our cause. Until he decided to run for the GOP nomination a few months ago, Trump had done none of these things, perhaps because he was too distracted publicly raising money for liberals such as the Clintons; championing Planned Parenthood, tax increases, and single-payer health coverage; and demonstrating his allegiance to the Democratic Party.

I stand by what I wrote, without apologies. It was true. It is also true that since taking the oath of office President Trump has walked with conservatives as well as Ronald Reagan and in some respects even more than the Gipper did.

However, Donald Trump did not care for what I wrote. Seven days later "the Great Brent" was on the receiving end of a patented Trump tweet.

> @BrentBozell, one of the National Review lightweights, came to my office begging for money like a dog. Why doesn't he say that?

Maybe because it wasn't true? I had not gone to him for money; he'd invited me for lunch to discuss his potential campaign. I hadn't groveled. I hadn't even asked for money. He'd offered it. That tweet was just another day at the office for Trump. I found myself laughing (my wife, Norma, found none of this humorous). It was going to be a wild and bumpy ride.

One by one Trump's sixteen competitors were vanquished, beginning with Jeb Bush and his $100 million war chest. Bush was the moderates' Chosen One, and the establishment was convinced he was unstoppable. Trump returned Jeb to the private sector brutally and immediately. Looking back, it should have been clear at that moment that this was The Year of Trump, and nothing was going to stop this juggernaut. Support for this candidate from his opponents' followers was by no means automatic, and from some quarters, like Governor John Kasich, virtually nonexistent.

But once the GOP convention was concluded and its nominee was chosen, it was time for the Republican nominee to turn his cannon fire on Hillary.

Some who had submitted pieces in that *National Review* issue joined the #NeverTrump ranks. I never joined. Like millions of other conservatives, I did not like the way Trump had conducted his primary campaign. I found the personal attacks distasteful in general. Some of the attacks on good men like Ted Cruz were repugnant. Even if Trump did not personally orchestrate them (i.e., the ultimate "fake news" story in *National Enquirer* linking Rafael Cruz to JFK's assassination), he did nothing to condemn them.

Trump the Entrepreneur promised to vastly reduce both corporate and personal tax rates while breaking the arrogant financial institutions—banks, insurance companies, defense contractors, and most especially the lobbyists servicing these entities—pillaging the US treasury. Fiscal conservatives were relishing the message, especially because it was coming from a billionaire businessman looking at America as a business itself.

Trump the Patriot energized the America First crowd. The promise to build the wall and halt the flow of unvetted immigrants, drug runners, and potential terrorists became the cornerstone of every speech. He was not only getting tough on America's enemies (finally!), he was getting tough on deadbeat allies (finally!). Most importantly, he was committing to rebuilding America's shattered defenses. Both military hawks and foreign policy isolationists were applauding.

Trump the Liberator wowed the libertarians. He was unequivocally declaring war on Washington, D.C., vowing to take a blow torch to regulations, beginning with the greatest federal disaster ever, Obamacare. He understood that while robbing Americans of their freedoms, these regulations were choking the life out of her economy. America needed a presidential Heimlich maneuver, and Trump was going to apply it. After 16 years of anemic growth (at best), very good times were almost here again.

Trump the Traditionalist emerged and the evangelicals were born yet again. He called for judges that would interpret, not rewrite the Constitution. That's standard fare for Republican presidential candidates, of course. But then he did what Romney never dared. And McCain never dared. And neither did 43. Ditto for Dole and before him Bush 41. In fact, not even candidate or President Reagan did it. Donald Trump announced, unequivocally, that he would name a *pro-life* Supreme Court justice, and even released his short list of candidates, all of them pro-lifers. It was the most significant pledge ever made to the pro-life movement (and one he would honor immediately with the nomination of Judge Neil Gorsuch).

Late into the night of November 8, Donald Trump pulled off one of the greatest upsets in modern political history. The man who had told me nineteen months before, "I really do think I can win this," and who registered 3 percent in the polls the day he announced his candidacy, was elected as the forty-fifth President of the United States.

It's been only two and a half years, and President Donald J. Trump has changed America and stunned the world.

On the domestic front he has honored one promise after another. Trump first delivered Supreme Court Justice Neil Gorsuch, then Brett Kavanaugh, another strict constructionist. He's cut taxes, the corporate ones dramatically, the domestic ones not so much, but combined the tax cuts have spurred a dramatic resurgence of the economy, aided also by an astonishing assault on the regulatory beast that has kept its paws firmly placed on the neck of corporate America, especially small business, for decades.

On the international front he's all but declared economic war on the nations, along with the European Union, that have been abusing this country for decades with tariffs that have made a mockery of free trade. Simultaneously, in a striking reversal from the tepid, or in the case of Iran, astonishingly accommodationist policies toward America's enemies,

Trump has broadcast a desire to be confrontational, speaking loudly and carrying an even bigger stick. His successful push to increase defense spending speaks volumes.

This is not to say that he's not had his share of defeats and promises unkept. The national debt is a national disgrace, and neither the GOP-controlled Congress, whose leadership and most of its members cannot be trusted, nor this administration have shown the courage to reduce it by a penny. All the posturing to the contrary, Obamacare still exists. The wall is unbuilt and underfunded. Planned Parenthood continues to receive money to kill babies. (It's fungible, folks.) Free traders believe that tariffs are a monumental mistake. He's now completed his second historic summit with Kim Jong-un and there's no denuclearizing in sight. Evidence still points to "Rocket Man" in relentless pursuit of an ever-expanding military threat against the United States. And then there's Russia, always Russia.

Trump should not be considered immune from valid criticism, and this book is not a whitewash. There are the policy and political shortcomings.

And then there are the unforced errors, mostly caused by his incessant—and so often plain obnoxious—tweeting. While his hardened base tends to embrace the tone of that which so readily offends the elites in Washington, D.C., New York City, and Tinseltown, even they shake their heads in disappointment at some of his targets. LeBron James? Arnold Schwarzenegger? Meryl Streep? The Freedom Caucus? Time and again we awake to read he's just viciously assaulted someone from the immensely popular to the thoroughly irrelevant, even his own friends and staff.

At the head of the so-called Resistance is the national so-called news media. It is the height of dishonesty that these "journalists" deny they have joined the far left in common cause and with undisguised brio. Today they are simply incapable of just reporting the news. They must be judgmental at all times. This bias is found in many ways. It is found in the story selected and the story ignored. It is found in the spokespersons quoted and the ones silenced. It's in the headlines and in the conclusions and everywhere in between.

Every elected Republican since Dwight Eisenhower—Nixon, Reagan, Bush 41, and Bush 43—has been treated with nothing but hostility. (Ford doesn't count. He was both unelected and too irrelevant for anyone to care.) The hostility extends to most GOP presidential candidates as well. Dozens in the last fifty years have been kneecapped by the news media in pursuit of their mission to elect their Democratic alternative.

But Trump is in a category of his own. The national news media were obsessed with the man from the start, laughing at the idea of this buffoon running and then, when his campaign was under way, ridiculing him at every opportunity, still dismissing any thought that he might win his party's nomination as his numbers continued to climb. When he became the nominee and posed a threat even they couldn't ignore, they waged scorched-earth warfare against him, breaking all the rules of journalistic ethics in a desperate attempt to change the outcome of the election. It wasn't that they thought he could win (they didn't). It was that he needed to be destroyed just in case. But he won, and they've been on a jihad ever since to remove him from office.

Trump is unique in another regard. As opposed to every other Republican who has ignored this enemy or, worse, fled for the tall grass in terror, from the start Donald J. Trump understood that the news media were his most powerful enemy, hell-bent on preventing his election and, when that failed, destroying his presidency.

So he went to war.

This is the story of a media that set out to destroy a president and his administration, but destroyed themselves instead.

L. Brent Bozell III

UNMASKED

1

The Inevitable Trump Loss
That Didn't Happen

JOURNALISTS ARE THE SMARTEST people in the room, so smart that they can't possibly be expected to just *report* the news. Thus, they grant themselves license to package it and analyze it with an intelligence only they seem to possess. They profess to believe in the power of facts, but what they really believe in is their power to proclaim facts. Facts exist to be bent to their will to further their narrative.

In 2016 that narrative was more an unequivocal declaration: Donald Trump must not win.

It was clear from the start that Donald Trump was itching for a fight with the media. He was going to put the entire profession on trial in the court of public opinion, and he did that by introducing two words that within a year had become part of the political lexicon: "fake news." The media were aghast that they would be so rudely challenged and dismissed the charges—angrily. Perhaps they had a point. It was certainly unfair to paint an entire institution with this broad, ugly brush. But when Trump unmasked one truly fake news story after another, the self-righteous press met the evidence with stony silence. The institution was guilty of aiding and abetting fake news. It still is.

The campaign didn't begin this way, however. When Trump descended the now-famous Trump Tower escalator and announced his candidacy to become the forty-fifth President of the United States, the announcement was met with ridicule. Trump wasn't just dead on arrival. He was a joke.

MSNBC host Andrea Mitchell asked Ed Rendell, the former Democratic governor of Pennsylvania: "Do you have any doubt that this is anything more than a carnival show?" Over on CNN, noontime anchor Ashleigh Banfield teased an upcoming segment on Trump's announcement by asking if it was "hilarity run amuck." CNN commentator S. E. Cupp called it "a rambling mess of a speech. . . . I was howling. Howling!"

On Bloomberg's daily political show *With All Due Respect*, co-host John Heilemann explained, "I do not hate Donald Trump, but I do not take him seriously. I thought, you know, everything that was garish and ridiculous about him was fully on display. . . . Will it get him anywhere close to becoming the nominee or the President of the United States? I think not."

PBS NewsHour anchor Judy Woodruff calmly relayed, "So far, Trump has placed near the bottom in public opinion polls of the Republican presidential hopefuls."

She was right to say that. He was tied for tenth at just 3 percent in a CNN poll of self-described Republicans (and independent-leaning Republicans), and that was where her colleagues thought he'd remain, too.

"He can't win, but he can get a lot of votes," *Washington Post* columnist E. J. Dionne, a former political reporter, predicted on MSNBC's *The Last Word.* The *Huffington Post*'s Marc Lamont Hill agreed over on CNN: "Of course he's not going to win." CBS correspondent Nancy Cordes echoed that opinion: "No one expects Trump to get close to winning the nomination."

The morning after Trump's announcement, MSNBC *Morning Joe* pundit Mike Barnicle chortled, "Can we stipulate for the purposes of this conversation that Donald Trump will never be President of the United States?"

CBS This Morning host Norah O'Donnell reported that "some Republicans say they're worried Trump will turn the campaign into a circus," and the subsequent story by correspondent Nancy Cordes cautioned that "party leaders worry Trump's presence will turn the primary into a joke."

NBC's *Today* relegated the news to a dismissive twenty-three-second brief but made sure to include this insulting sentence: "America's largest Latino civil rights organization called Trump 'an exceedingly silly man.'"

That night, NBC's evening newscast took it to the next level, featuring a rare narrated piece by *Meet the Press* moderator Chuck Todd, who unloaded on Trump. "On the one hand, he's a late-night joke," he stated. "On the other, he's the proverbial skunk at the garden party. How does the Republican Party handle a political streaker who knows how to get attention?"

With "moderators" like this, who needed left-wing Democratic Party spokespersons?

The Associated Press rounded up all the delighted late-night comedians as part of its "news" coverage. ABC's Jimmy Kimmel joked that Trump would be like a "president and an amusement park all rolled up into one." NBC's Seth Meyers said that "in a speech cobbled together from forwarded emails from your uncle, he let us know what he thought that America needed." Despite leaving *The Daily Show*, Jon Stewart released a video calling the announcement speech "over a half-hour of the most beautifully ridiculous jibber-jabber ever to pour forth from the mouth" of a billionaire.

On Bloomberg TV's *With All Due Respect*, co-host John Heilemann acknowledged that all this carried a whiff of elitism: "For the national press corps and other elites, Donald Trump's campaign is a pure vanity exercise, and a target ripe for outright mockery, or low-level derision."

Translation: Viewed through the eyes of his colleagues, only single-toothed welfare inbreds with second-grade educations could vote for Donald Trump.

The mockery and derision have never stopped. The media had to be dragged kicking and screaming to the realization that a large segment of Americans wasn't listening to their chattering. In fact, these nonstop insult barrages were galvanizing his supporters.

We acknowledge that it would seem easy to dismiss Trump's chances in the Republican primaries if you were looking at this through the lens of traditional electoral politics. He had never run for any political office and was certainly rough around the edges, to be kind. He was loud and obnoxious, the polar opposite of presidential timber. Pundits looked at the gravitas and experience, the fund-raising process and endless endorsements, and the brand names of candidates such as Jeb Bush and Hillary Clinton and expected them to land the two nominations for those reasons. Indeed, these were foregone conclusions for most reporters. The "experts" were about to be exposed as dinosaurs, thoroughly out of touch with the American electorate.

On the first night, Trump's announcement captured just four and a half minutes of airtime on the ABC, CBS, and NBC evening newscasts. NBC made Trump the third story. CBS waited until the sixth story. ABC made it the ninth item of the night.

To put that level of uninterest in its proper perspective, compare that with their coverage of the last president's announcement. When Barack Hussein Obama announced his presidential bid on February 10, 2007, he too was an outsider without endorsements or branding, and he was registering just 18 percent in the polls, far behind the pre-sumed nominee, Hillary. Yet the same reporters covered it as an inspirational moment in American history. He didn't need to have a long résumé. In fact, he had no accomplish-ments. But he was black, a radical leftist, and charismatic, and so his self-narrated life story (including a memoir full of casual lies) was enough to qualify him as the next leader of the free world.

The day Obama announced, they went nuts for him.

Both ABC and NBC led their evening broadcasts with the Obama story even though it had been anticipated for months. CBS had scrapped its newscast, preferring to run sports instead, but its *Saturday Early Show* made up for it. They previewed it by devoting *over nine minutes* of "breaking news" time to Obama's decision. It included *Politico*'s Mike Allen quipping, "Senator Obama has gotten such great publicity all his life that one of his friends joked to me that this morning, he's throwing his halo into the ring." So true. (And just imagine how Hillary must have responded to this coverage! No lamp in whatever room she was in was safe that night.)

Still, this was their dream, not their reality. She still had it in the bag. Shortly after that day we were in the green room at Fox preparing to do the Hannity show. Asked what chance Obama stood, former Clinton advisor Dick Morris echoed the media's outlook on the 2008 presidential election outcome: "You conservatives are going to have to face reality. The next President of the United States of America *will* be Hillary Clinton."

Democratic campaigns often are described in happy word pictures provided by "close friends" of the candidates. Liberals are awarded gold stars and twenty extra IQ points just for being liberals. They promise "hope" and "change" and never have to define what it means, knowing that their friends in the media will never call them out. But conservatives? They are presumed to be either evil or stupid and sometimes both. Anyone around in 1968, 1976, 1980, and 1984—the years Ronald Reagan ran for president—will remember that.

Donald Trump made it clear that his days as a liberal Democrat were behind him. Like Reagan, Trump declared he was now a conservative Republican. Now the leftist press was going to despise not just his personality but his policies, too.

Right off the bat they erupted over his comments about illegal immigrants from Mexico: "They're bringing drugs, they're bringing crime. They're rapists. And some, I assume, are good people." In the first month of his campaign, ABC, CBS and NBC aired a combined thirty-one evening news stories discussing this comment ad nauseam. It would be so, one controversial statement after the next, throughout the campaign. Trump thoroughly controlled the news cycle.

Trump opponents on both sides of the partisan divide kept finding moments when they just knew his campaign would self-destruct. The opening speech about Mexico sending rapists. The statements that John McCain was a loser for getting captured in Vietnam. The presumed resistance to filling out any financial disclosure forms. Daring to withhold his tax returns. Pledging to suspend Muslim immigration to the United States. Slamming the federal judge who ordered the release of Trump Foundation documents as a "Mexican" when he was Mexican-American. Attacking grieving Muslim Gold Star parents who criticized him from the stage of the Democratic convention. Finally, there was the supposed silver bullet: the 2005 Billy Bush *Access Hollywood* tape, bragging about grabbing women.

Every misstep of the way they believed—hoped—he was a dead candidate walking, yet to their horror he seemed only to gain steam, with packed arenas and tens of thousands standing outside watching jumbotrons, roaring their approval along with millions doing the same thing at home. But it wasn't just the maverick nature of this man and the unorthodox campaign he was running. It was the message. The press had no idea how powerfully it was resonating.

Missing the Revolution

The smartest people in the room believe their thumbs are pressed firmly on the pulse of the American public, but their world extends only across a tract of land along the Manhattan–Washington, D.C., corridor, along with some real estate in Beverly Hills. They were clueless as to the mood of an electorate in the real America that has lost its patience with the elites both in and out of government. This necessarily included them.

To understand the electorate in 2016 it is essential that one (re)read Angelo Codevilla's "America's Ruling Class— And the Perils of Revolution," published by *The American Spectator* six years before. The 12,000-word essay was a masterpiece, read out loud by Rush Limbaugh to his millions of listeners. Codevilla presented an existential struggle for the future of America between what he dubbed the "ruling class" and the "country class." It was prescient. Codevilla had perfectly described the opposing forces in the 2016 presidential campaign.

The ruling class is a fraternity whose membership includes those in a position of power over a population it views as less able—if not wholly unable—to handle its own affairs. "For our ruling class, America is a work in progress, just like the rest of the world, and they are the engineers." The ruling class has no party affiliation. "Differences between Bushes, Clintons, and Obamas are of degrees, not kind," the author wrote. "No prominent Republican challenge[s] the ruling class's claim of superior insight, nor its denigration of the American people as irritable children who must learn their place. The Republican Party [does] not disparage the ruling class, because most of its officials are or would like to be part of it."

On the other side of the coin is the country class with its "desire to get rid of rulers it regards inept and haughty. . . . The country class is convinced that big business, big government, and big finance are linked as never before and that ordinary people are more unequal than ever. . . . The country class actually believes that America's ways are superior to the rest of the world's, and regards most of mankind as less free, less prosperous, and less virtuous."

Trump fundamentally understood the divide, and the billionaire chose to champion the country class. That would necessarily pit him against virtually all levels of power in America today: against the establishment elite of both political parties, against the Chamber of Commerce oligarchy, against the unions, against academia, against Hollywood, and of course against the national news media.

Interestingly enough, the country class uprising Codevilla had identified wasn't limited to the United States. The same phenomenon was emerging in other nations. Many of the same issues, including unfair trade practices, uncontrolled illegal immigration, and Islamic terrorism, were triggering populist uprisings, and just as with the Trump phenomenon, the American news media chose sides.

It started with the elections in Israel on March 17.

The manufactured conventional wisdom and polling predicted a tight race and rough sledding for conservative prime minister Benjamin Netanyahu. NPR's Emily Harris reported from Jerusalem, "We might not know for days or even weeks who the next prime minister of Israel will actually be." Instead the conservative won quickly and decisively, and that triggered a media explosion with the usual sore-loser outbursts about racist campaign tactics and how Mideast peace was dead. CNN anchor Christiane Amanpour channeled the hostility of Arab Israelis who, she said, "feel that the Likud Party and the right wing do have a, sort of, racist policy towards them and it's very scary for them."

Ring a bell?

Next came the British parliamentary elections on May 7. On NBC's *Meet the Press* on May 3, host Chuck Todd proclaimed the race between Conservative Party prime minister David Cameron and Labour Party leftist Ed Miliband "too close to call." Channeling the usual Democrat analysts, Todd declared, "There's been commentary that if Cameron loses, the Republican Party ought to learn something from that."

On MSNBC, anchor Andrea Mitchell brought on "senior political analyst" David Axelrod to make a fool of himself: "I think that the polls are accurate. This is a very, very close race, highly likely that this drama extends beyond tonight." Wrong on both counts. Cameron defied the "experts" and won a clear majority in Parliament.

Like Obama field organizer Jeremy Bird, who had worked diligently in Israel to defeat Netanyahu only to fail, Axelrod had traveled to London to work for Labour, and like a good Obama strategist, he blamed others for the failure of his predictions: "In all my years as journalist & strategist, I've never seen as stark a failure of polling as in UK. Huge project ahead to unravel that."

The defeats for the ruling class just kept coming. In June, the media were shocked again when Britain voted to leave the European Union—for a "Brexit"—over trade and immigration concerns. As in Israel, Team Obama was meddling with Britain's country class, with Obama writing an op-ed against Brexit that appeared while he was visiting England in April. Only CBS quoted British politicians such as like Boris Johnson criticizing the interference. "The U.S. guards its democracy with more hysterical jealousy than any other country on Earth," he stated. "It's a breathtaking example of do as I say, not as I do."

Speaking of breathtaking, the *New York Times* actually complained that British tabloids were "pushing an agenda," dwelling on their "nationalist and anti-European tendencies." As another omen of things to come in the States, the "Remain" [in the EU] side on the center-left led in the polls, but the polls were wrong, and the "Leave" side won, 52 percent to 48 percent.

How to explain the inaccurate polls? Fox Business anchor Stuart Varney argued that people had been intimidated by the elites and were loath to express their beliefs publicly: "People who wanted to get out of the European Union were shamed into saying 'Well, I'm not sure. Maybe we should stay.' Because, in Britain if you wanted to get out, you were labeled a bigot. You were labeled an Islamophobe. You didn't like foreigners. You were a hater."

The media's reaction to the Brexit victory confirmed Varney's theory. Over at the *New York Times* they were especially nauseated by the results. Columnist Roger Cohen said Brexit was a "colossal leap in the dark," and columnist Paul

Krugman called for readers to "grieve for Europe." Michael Kimmelman, the architecture critic, announced the Brexit polling didn't capture enough hate. It was "a clear signal, albeit not surprisingly, for increased skepticism when it comes to all polling that involves xenophobia and racism."

Julie Bort at the *Business Insider* website summed it up for the ruling class: "Britain is broken beyond repair and the ignorant are officially running the world." A *Financial Times* editor tweeted, "I picked the wrong day to stop sniffing glue!"

Trump, the Race-Baiting, Clinically Insane, Neo-Fascist Sociopath

All of this was an early indicator of how badly the elites were going to misjudge Trump. They dismissed him as an unsavory character. They missed the uprising he was leading. In the infamous Republican debate on CNBC in the fall of 2015, lead moderator John Harwood began by asking Trump: "Let's be honest. Is this a comic book version of a presidential campaign?" But Harwood wasn't alone. The other CNBC "moderators" got into the act and proceeded to ridicule one GOP candidate after the next, until Senator Ted Cruz reached the end of his tether over their nonstop insults: "The questions asked so far in this debate illustrate why the American people don't trust the media. . . . You look at the questions. Donald Trump, are you a comic book villain? Ben Carson, can you do math? John Kasich, can you insult those two people over here? Marco Rubio, will you resign? Jeb Bush, why have your numbers fallen? How about talking about the substantive issues people care about?" The audience roared its approval. The CNBC crew returned to Washington, D.C., and New York thoroughly humiliated, a case study on how to completely screw up a national debate.

CBS's *Face the Nation* brought on *Slate* writer Jamelle Bouie to smear Trump voters as racist: "Trump's supporters show all the hallmarks of people with high levels of racial resentment. They are—you know, they seem—a good number believe that President Obama is un-American or maybe even a Muslim and connected to terrorists. A good number referred to him as arrogant and elitist which, for myself, reads very much like 'uppity' as an old insult towards African Americans who have achieved some sort of stature in mainstream society."

PBS host Tavis Smiley threw the race card with more velocity on ABC's *This Week*: "Trump is still, to my mind at least, an unrepentant, irascible, religious and racial arsonist," he screamed. "And so, when we talk about how Trump is rising in the polls, you can't do that absent the kind of campaign he's running, the issues he's raising."

As Trump's chances of winning the nomination grew, the historical analogies grew more ridiculous—and offensive. On February 26, the *Washington Post* editorial board decided to compare Trump's proposed crackdown on illegal immigration to murderers of millions: "He would round up and deport 11 million people, a forced movement on a scale not attempted since Stalin or perhaps Pol Pot. . . . He routinely trades in wild falsehoods and doubles down when his lies are exposed." The *Post*'s editorial writers repeated this Pol Pot slur (equating deportation and execution) on April 22: "Remember that Mr. Trump promised to round up 11 million undocumented immigrants and deport them, in what would be the largest forced population movement since Pol Pot's genocide of the Cambodian people."

CNN commentator Sally Kohn lit some warning flares of her own. Even if you couldn't vote for Hillary, "the woman who's running with the impeccable and vast record of experience, if that's not enough for people, at least stopping us from being Nazi Germany would hopefully get Democrats and others to turn out." CNN anchor Alisyn Camerota left the Nazi smear unchallenged. Three days later on CNN, Kohn drove the hyperbole into Fantasyland. She worried: "When he [Trump] institutes internment camps and suspends *habeas*, we'll all look back and feel pretty bad."

The Nazi smears were all the rage for the outraged. *New York Times* columnist David Brooks cracked on *Meet the Press*: "If we're going to get Trump, we might as well get the Nuremberg rallies to go with it!"

George Stephanopoulos threw Hitler at Trump on *Good Morning America*. "The number of prominent people comparing you to Adolf Hitler is actually growing by the day. . . . I can't remember that kind of comparison being used against any other presidential candidate. Does it suggest to you that you should tone down your rhetoric and your tactics?"

CNN host Erin Burnett badgered Florida's Republican governor, Rick Scott. "The current president of Mexico—two former presidents of Mexico—have compared him to Hitler," she said. "Vicente Fox, former president, specifically said, 'He reminds me of Hitler.' It's direct. It's not an allusion. It's a direct thing. 'He reminds me of Hitler.' Do they have a point?"

By March 15, Trump had won nineteen of the first twenty-nine state primaries or caucuses and his opponents were dropping like flies. Jeb Bush had spent $100 million fruitlessly. Marco Rubio, Ben Carson, and Rand Paul were also gone. So too were Jim Gilmore, Chris Christie, Carly Fiorina, Rick Santorum, Mike Huckabee, George Pataki, Lindsey Graham, Bobby Jindal, Scott Walker, and Rick Perry. All that remained were John Kasich and Ted Cruz, his most serious challenger.

By May 13, as Trump closed in on the nomination, NPR's *On the Media* host Bob Garfield lost control of his metaphors and, for a moment, his mind. Trump's "supposedly courageous candor is contaminated with the most cowardly hate speech—racism, xenophobia, misogyny, incitement, breathtaking ignorance on issues, both foreign and domestic, and a nuclear recklessness, reminiscent of a raving meth-head with a machete on an episode of *Cops*."

Trump was no longer a joke. He was a threat, and once the leftists convinced themselves Trump was a national menace, it wasn't long before some of them started talking up violence. The *Huffington Post* published an article by Jesse Benn on June 6, 2016, headlined "Sorry, Liberals, a Violent Response to Trump Is as Logical as Any." Benn argued: "In the face of media, politicians, and GOP primary voters normalizing Trump as a presidential candidate—whatever your personal beliefs regarding violent resistance—there's an inherent value in forestalling Trump's normalization. Violent resistance accomplishes this."

Benn wasn't kidding. After a radical leftist gunned down Congressman Steve Scalise and several others in June 2017,

Benn tweeted the shooter some advice: "For violent resistance to work, it'd need to be organized. Individual acts can be understandable, but likely counterproductive/ineffective."

Then there was the army of amateur psychiatrists. On June 8, 2016, CBS contributor Nancy Giles insisted to MSNBC host Lawrence O'Donnell that Trump was "clinically insane." O'Donnell agreed. "You're not alone," he responded. "There's a lot of clinicians who have been speculating about that." Unsurprisingly for O'Donnell, he didn't produce a single name.

New York Times columnist Andrew Rosenthal, a former editorial page editor at the paper, loathed Trump's proposed travel ban from Muslim countries that support terrorism. "Let's be absolutely clear," he lectured. "This is not just about bigotry. The mass arrest and forced movement of large populations has been an instrument of genocide throughout history. That is how the Turks committed genocide against Armenians in the early 20th century, how the United States government decimated some Native American tribes and how Stalin killed millions of his own citizens."

In a July 12, 2016, interview with *Rolling Stone* magazine, which is not a place you should go for journalistic integrity and truth telling, MSNBC host Rachel Maddow saw the Führer in Trump's eyes. "What's the worst-case scenario for America if he [Donald Trump] wins? It can be pretty bad. You don't have to go back far in history to get to almost apocalyptic scenarios. . . . Over the past year I've been reading a lot about what it was like when Hitler first became chancellor. I am gravitating toward moments in history for subliminal reference in terms of cultures that have unexpectedly veered into dark places, because I think that's possibly where we are."

Legendary *Washington Post* reporter turned crackpot Carl Bernstein kept dropping the political F-word on Trump, as in this CNN interview snippet on October 21, 2016: "This campaign is now about a neo-fascist—I keep coming back to that—sociopath. . . . He is setting himself up as the head of . . . a real neo-fascist movement. . . . Is there going to be remnants of a neo-fascist movement that he leads in this country after this election? It's a dangerous thing. We're in a dangerous place."

Trump was now a racist, a xenophobe, a misogynist, an ignoramus, a neo-fascist, and a sociopath, all rolled into one, clearly a menace and a threat to the future of the United States, if not humankind itself. But one thing was also for certain. It wasn't going to happen in 2016. The media, like virtually everyone else on the left, were still utterly convinced Hillary had this one in the bag.

The Angry Aftermath: A "Moral 9/11"

As the campaign entered the final days, the media's overconfidence in a Clinton victory was everywhere. On MSNBC, Chris Matthews was gleefully reading from one of those anonymously sourced *Washington Post* reports: "A wave of apprehension and anguish swept the Republican Party on Thursday, with many GOP leaders concluding it is probably too late to salvage his flailing presidential campaign. Republicans privately acknowledge it could be a landslide victory for Democratic nominee Hillary Clinton."

A few days later, *CBS Evening News* anchor Scott Pelley proclaimed, "Time is running out for Donald Trump. . . . No candidate down this far, this late has ever recovered." Two days later, ABC's Jon Karl warned, "Donald Trump is down

17 points among women. You do not get elected president of the United States if you are down 17 points among women." On MSNBC's *The Last Word with Lawrence O'Donnell, Washington Post* columnist Eugene Robinson gushed over a Florida poll that claimed that 28 percent of Republicans were voting for Clinton and declared that "if it's anywhere near that then this election, not only that Florida fall to Hillary Clinton but this election overall could, you know—we could be talking landslide." (Trump won Florida.)

With six days to go, former Bush and McCain staffer Nicolle Wallace insisted she was bringing the "cold hard truth" to the table on NBC: "The best case scenario, if [Trump and Co.] do everything right? They lose with 266 electoral votes."

On the Sunday before the election, ABC political analyst Matthew Dowd (another former Bushie) called it for Hillary. "She's got about a 95 percent chance in this election, and I think she's going to have a higher margin than Barack Obama in 2012."

The *Huffington Post* proclaimed that Hillary Clinton was 98 percent likely to defeat Trump.

Ryan Grim of *HuffPost* argued, "It's not easy to sit here and tell you that Clinton has a 98 percent chance of winning. Everything inside us screams out that life is too full of uncertainty, that being so sure is just a fantasy. But that's what the numbers say." Grim later repeated, "If you want to put your faith in the numbers, you can relax. She's got this."

On the morning of Election Day, Eleanor Clift was measuring the drapes for a woman president in the *Daily Beast*: "There are likely to be more than 20 women in the Senate after Tuesday, and together with Clinton in the White House, they will send a strong signal to women and girls that nothing is holding them back, that the future is there for them."

This arrogant, elitist overconfidence is precisely what made election night so enjoyable for Trump voters. On the *CBS Evening News* shortly before the polls began to close, reporter Nancy Cordes claimed that after being "dogged by her e-mail troubles, a restless electorate, and an unorthodox opponent," Clinton aides insisted Hillary's "perseverance through all of it, Scott, shows she's prepared for the nation's toughest job."

As ABC's prime-time election night coverage began, they turned to former evening-news anchor Charles Gibson, who promptly whacked Trump for not being as classy as his opponent, referring to Hillary Clinton's 2014 memoir *Hard Choices*: "The chapter about when you should apologize, I think Donald Trump missed that chapter somewhere along the line."

Every single major news outlet picked Hillary Clinton to win a month before the election. Ironically, one of the worst prognosticators was Fox News. On the October 21 edition of *Special Report*, Bret Baier proclaimed that Hillary was going to trounce The Donald. The FNC electoral map had her winning the Electoral College 307–181, with 50 toss-up votes.

But on election night things weren't going according to the script. Hillary was supposed to pick up some red states while sweeping the battleground states. She was supposed to win Florida early, which would seal the deal—but she lost. She was supposed to capture North Carolina—but she lost. "As Ohio goes, so goes the nation," and she was going to pick up that state—but she lost that one too. A shell-shocked national media saw the impossible developing. And then the roof caved in when blue states considered impregnable by the pundits started to fall. First Pennsylvania, then Wisconsin, and then, sealing the deal, Michigan.

Donald J. Trump had been elected the forty-fifth President of the United States.

Liberals found themselves talking to themselves. They tried being temporarily apologetic on NBC, with Chuck Todd admitting that "we have overlooked rural America a bit too much." Former anchor Tom Brokaw backhanded Trump's voters as miscreants who "have to pull a pin on a grenade and roll it across the country, whatever it takes. 'We want change, and we want big change!'" Leftist journalism professor Jeff Jarvis at New York University hyperventilated, choosing to blame the media for not being harsh enough: "I fear that journalism is irredeemably broken, a failure. My profession failed to inform the public about the fascist they are electing." Just as New York University fails to teach journalism when it employs the likes of Jeff Jarvis.

It was the same thing with comedians on election night. What was supposed to be a knee-slapping funfest became no laughing matter. Expecting a Hillary Clinton victory, CBS late-night host Stephen Colbert was given an hour on CBS-owned Showtime for a we-won trash-talk special. They titled it *Stephen Colbert's Live Election Night Democracy's Series Finale: Who's Going to Clean Up This Shit?* Colbert came out to a big standing ovation and cracked, "Please have a seat. You don't need to stand for me. You don't need to chant my name. America doesn't have dictators . . . yet!" But then a worried Colbert proclaimed that the race was far too close: "This one is a nail biter and a passport grabber. It feels like we are trying to avoid the apocalypse and half the country is voting for the asteroid."

As the real possibility of a Trump upset began to unfold, panic hit the set. Comedy Central *Daily Show* host Trevor Noah was in full hysteria, telling Colbert: "I don't know if you've come to the right place for jokes tonight. Because this is the first time throughout this entire race where I'm officially shitting my pants! I genuinely do not understand how America can be this disorganized or this hateful!"

Comedian Jena Friedman picked up on Colbert's voting-for-the-asteroid metaphor: "It feels like an asteroid has just smacked into our democracy! It is so scary and sad and heart-breaking and I just wish I could be funny. Get your abortions now because we're going to be fucked and we're going to have to live with it!"

MSNBC hosts Mark Halperin and John Heilemann (who also had a Showtime election series called *The Circus*) were on scene to add expert analysis to the comedy. Halperin clearly lost control as he wildly proclaimed, "Outside of the Civil War and World War II, and including 9/11, this may be the most cataclysmic event the country's ever seen!" Colbert cooed his appreciation, "I'm so glad you guys are here. I wouldn't want to be alone right now." In the midnight hour, CNN analyst (and former Obama White House aide) Van Jones took to crying racism in defeat: "It's hard to be a parent, tonight, for a lot of us. You tell your kids, 'Don't be a bully.' You tell your kids, 'Don't be a bigot. . . .' And then, you have this outcome. . . . How do I explain this to my children? This was a 'white-lash.' This was a 'white-lash' against a changing country. It was a 'white-lash' against a black president."

National Public Radio was still in anger mode after the election on Wednesday's *Morning Edition* news program, bringing on black author Attica Locke (who also writes for the Fox drama *Empire*), who rudely implied that each and every Trump supporter is a racist. NPR anchor David Greene politely suggested that it was not every one of them, but Locke refused to concede that there was a single nonracist: "I'm out with that. There's a part of me that honestly feels like that level of politeness, where we're not calling things what they are, is how we will never get forward." Locke then went on Twitter to promote her taxpayer-funded radio rant: "Me on the election on NPR. The 'R' word is the new 'N' word, I guess. Why are folks afraid to say racist?" *NBC Nightly News* correspondent Richard Engel chronicled a global panic on the Wednesday night after Trump won: "There were gasps around the world. Headlines, 'Trumpocalypse' and 'Disunited States.' And echoes of the Brexit vote too, against the European Union establishment. But there are deeper concerns tonight that the world's shining light of democracy has gone dark."

New York Times columnist Thomas Friedman echoed Halperin's 9/11 metaphor on Friday night on HBO's *Real Time with Bill Maher*: "This is a moral 9/11! Only 9/11 was done to us from the outside and we did this to ourselves." Hillary losing was now the moral equivalent of losing 3,000 Americans in a terrorist attack.

That verdict came after Maher's own angry rant against Trump voters, who he believed had sealed their own doom: "Enjoy your victory, Trump voters. Because when you're dying because you don't have health insurance to treat the infection you got for a back alley abortion you had to get because of fetal lead poisoning, you can say to yourself, at least I didn't vote for someone with a private e-mail server."

When Democrats win, it's a victory for hope and change and national unity. When Republicans win, it is a sad day, a victory for dark forces, their vicious lies and flagrant fouls, manipulating the unruly throng. As Peter Jennings infamously said after the 1994 Republican wave election, it was "a nation full of uncontrolled two-year-old rage," a stomping, screaming temper tantrum, not a serious verdict on the future of America. These voters would need to see the error of their ways and know the damage they had committed.

They saw Trump's voters just as the Clinton campaign saw them: a basket of deplorables. All season long the pro-Hillary press treated Trump's followers with utter contempt. This was the country class showing its utter temerity in challenging the ruling class. These were extra-chromosomed rednecks in MAGA hats. As Hillary put it, they were "irredeemable, but thankfully they are not America."

But those deplorables carried the day.

The pundits got it all wrong. They had accepted the comforting prophecies of the national media, not just regarding the coronation of Hillary Clinton, but on America's repudiation of Donald Trump. It was a resounding rejection of the ruling class—themselves. But these elites were not going silently into the night. The media would only double down, and triple down, and quadruple down as Trump made his way to the White House. All the rules learned at journalism school were tossed aside. If the news was harmful to this man, it was to be magnified; if it was favorable to him, it was to be ignored; and if needed, the "news" was faked.

The ruling class was not about to concede an inch of turf to the peasants.

2

Defining Our Terms

THERE IS NOTHING THAT inflames media elites more than Donald Trump dismissing them as fake news. It's not a criticism of a specific reporter, or a story, or even an outlet. It's a blanket condemnation of an entire industry. Worse, he's pinning this charge on what they believe to be above reproach because journalists are founts of truth, and woe to the man who challenges their integrity. They decide what is truth, and no one else.

Yet fake news exists. It has for a very long time.

In print, we think of Janet Cooke at the *Washington Post* who was awarded a Pulitzer Prize in 1981 for her shocking story of Jimmy the eight-year-old cocaine addict, except she'd made the whole thing up. We think of Jayson Blair at the *New York*

Times in 2003 pretending to report from Iraq War veteran Jessica Lynch's tiny West Virginia hometown when he was sitting in a bar down the street from Times Square.

On television, we think of NBC rigging GM trucks to explode on cue and ABC producers with hidden cameras trying to put rotten meat on sale at Food Lion. We think of Dan Rather spreading around phony National Guard memos to destroy George W. Bush's presidential campaign or Brian Williams claiming he was on a helicopter that took rocket fire during the Iraq War or making up scenes of floating bodies in the hurricane-flooded streets of New Orleans.

The flagrant fakery usually is cooked up in the service of a liberal goal because the ends justify the means. One could guess that some stories are "too good to check" when a liberal argument can be made. Or one could be more cynical and suggest that since most political news is created with the liberal agenda in mind, it's not surprising that some or all of that liberal product allows fraudulent claims as long as it propels the narrative. For Trump, the goal is to build a case for his removal from office.

Trump's critics will point out that he has a history of pushing his own fake news. He can be reckless with conspiracy theories. He toyed for years with the unproven charge that Barack Obama was born in Kenya. (As opposed to Obama's fairy tale that his father hung around with him in Hawaii until he was two, when actually his mother took him back to the mainland within a month of his birth.) During the primary campaign, Trump's friends at the *National Enquirer* used grainy old black-and-white photos to suggest that Ted Cruz's father "was with Lee Harvey Oswald" before the assassination of John F. Kennedy, and Trump made no effort to denounce the slander. He also bragged about a level of wealth that no serious analyst believes. His willingness to play loose with false information—or create it himself—adds a layer of outrage within the sanctimonious press.

National media leaders insist that they should be honored and respected as the arbiters of fact. Many stories on television and in print contain facts, but they also carry a lot of opinions that masquerade as facts, such as the "fact" that the Clintons are innocent every time they're caught in a lie—or criminal act. Facts can be spun. Or be nonexistent. Or be counterfeit.

It's a matter of degree. There is biased news, false news, and fake news.

Biased news appears when the facts or the sources of a story are arranged to deliver a particular perspective that is in keeping with the opinions of the author. It is an everyday phenomenon in the press—everywhere. In fact, one can argue that *all* news is biased. It starts with the decision to label something as news. Look at the front pages of the *Washington Post* and the *Washington Times* on any given day and you'll find a wide discrepancy in story selection. Each paper can defend its choice of "front-page" stories. But that judgment was predicated on subjective opinions, and that is bias.

That same bias is found in numerous other ways inside a story. The headline. The people interviewed and the length given to them. The tone of the questions. The edited responses. The conclusion reached. Bias, bias, bias.

A good reporter understands this. A good reporter seeks truth and commits to putting aside his or her prejudices—no easy task—in the process.

When President George H. W. Bush died and President Trump attended a memorial service at the National Cathedral with the former presidents, the *Washington Post* put Trump's discomfort on the front page under the headline "Despite Sitting with Predecessors, Trump Stands Alone at Funeral." Reporter Philip Rucker placed Trump in a mortifying spot: "First was the president Trump said was illegitimate (Barack Obama); then the first lady he called a profligate spender of taxpayer dollars (Michelle Obama); then the president he called the worst abuser of women (Bill Clinton); then the first lady and secretary of state he said should be in jail (Hillary Clinton); and then the president he said was the second-worst behind Obama (Jimmy Carter) and his wife, Rosalynn." Rucker had no space to counter this with the choice epithets Obama or the Clintons or the Carters lobbed at Trump.

On the same day, the *Washington Times* put Trump's attendance on page A-9 under the headline "With Trump on Fringes, Presidents Club Assembles to Attend Bush Funeral." It was an Associated Press dispatch that noted that both sides were hostile, not just one: "But the staid group of Oval Office occupants has been disturbed since Donald Trump's election. And since his swearing-in, Mr. Trump has spurned most contact with his predecessors—and they have snubbed him in return."

False news is when media outlets make a mistake. Sadly, this is where the arrogance of the press rears its ugly head. Like Fonzie from the old TV show *Happy Days*, they seem clinically unable to declare they were wr-wr-wr-wrong. And a correction? Not on your life.

After the Benghazi consulate attack in 2012, the Obama administration shamelessly tried to argue that the killing of four Americans was not a terrorist attack but a protest of an Islamophobic video on YouTube. The networks ran this argument for days . . . until the facts overwhelmed the White House talking points. The networks made a mistake and eventually corrected it. But then when Brian Williams had a chance to press President Obama on this false claim, he merely asked, "Have you been happy with the intelligence?" What mattered was whether Obama was *pleased*, not whether he mangled the facts.

Fake news is the inexcusable and the essence of journalistic dishonesty. The journalist knows that what he or she is presenting is either false or designed to advance an agenda. In 2004, Dan Rather had his producer Mary Mapes deliberately gather testimony from a Bush-hating malcontent pushing forged documents, ignoring document authenticators while deliberately refusing to interview firsthand witnesses from the Texas Air National Guard who would say the opposite because they wanted to sink Bush's reelection with the fake Air National Guard story. To this day, Rather insists that the "truth" was on their side and "We have to somehow get back to integrity in the news." The carelessness of the reporting underlined the malignant intentions.

Whether a news item is false or fake is only a matter of intentions. Neither is reliable information and as a result undermines confidence in the media outlet offering the reporting. When people suspect an ideological motivation behind a "news" report, they lose trust in the authenticity of what they see and hear from those "nonpartisan" journalists.

With Trump the ideological opposition was (and still is) so militant in its "reporting" that when he labeled it all fake news, his supporters were ready to accept that.

Some suggest that he might use a less combative synonym for "fake." Maybe "artificial" or "contrived." But why? When a reporter invents facts, she should be shamed publicly. Individually or collectively, when news outlets set the agenda for public discussion and tell us what we all should be talking about and how we should view that issue and it's all predicated on a lie, they deserve to be punished severely in the court of public opinion. When reporters continue to promote the line that Michael Brown in Ferguson, Missouri, had raised his hands and said to a policeman, "Hands up, don't shoot," knowing a thorough investigation found that he'd done no such thing, they deserved to be publicly humiliated.

Fake news is also thematic. "News" often is based on slippery underlying assumptions. The Ferguson falsehood projected a belief that white Southerners are naturally racist, and so too are opponents of immigration, and the same should be said about cops. However, the media's same assumptions about minorities—in their case, their victimhood—cause them deliberately to suppress news that might make people assume that Muslims are more likely to be terrorists or avoid reporting on black-on-black violence in big cities. That narrative isn't "helpful."

The term "fake news" resonates with Trump voters because people are frustrated with arrogant media elites dictating to them what is and isn't an acceptable belief system. For eight years of the Clintons and eight years of the Obamas, they saw these self-righteous watchdogs deliberately seek to avoid every Democratic scandal. Each example was "not news." But when there's just a whiff of wrongdoing on the other side—hold the presses! The Republican is always found guilty until he can prove his innocence, and even that won't be enough.

Since they first developed a taste for their own power in opposing the Vietnam War and forcing Richard Nixon to resign in the Watergate scandal, our national news corporations have become increasingly bold in picking winners and losers, explicitly telling voters who they must elect and what "landmark" legislation they must support. When the people fail in their election choices, they are compared to toddlers throwing tantrums. To repeat Peter Jennings' 1994 quote in its entirety, "Imagine a nation full of uncontrolled two-year-old rage. The voters had a temper tantrum last week."

The media then try to run the country between the elections, to enlighten obstreperous citizens, the "poor, uneducated, and easy-to-command" types. If they fail in stopping a man's cause, they cock the trigger and then fire the final bullet: character assassination. The goal is for your values to become as radioactive in the court of public opinion as the man or cause you supported.

As the media became more aggressive in their pursuit of a liberal agenda, with equal passion conservatives who saw through this plastic propaganda rushed to embrace alternative forms of media as they emerged. First it was Rush Limbaugh and conservative talk radio. The left's hostility to these uppity conservatives has never waned. Then Fox News emerged on television and overnight became the number one cable news network, so Fox News became Fake News. Leftists wore T-shirts with the Fox News logo and "Faux

News" painted on them, along with the slogan "We Distort, You Comply." They also sold shirts that read "I don't watch Fox News for the same reason I don't eat out of the toilet." They wanted people to cast a strange look at their relatives at the Thanksgiving table when they offered "news" that hadn't been mentioned on ABC, CBS, NBC, or CNN. News wasn't "reality" until the preposterously titled "mainstream media" gave it their stamp of approval.

For conservatives there is neither fairness nor balance, nor do the elites believe there should be. These journalists sit on the far left of the ideological spectrum, but they declare themselves centrists, and so virtually all things conservative are "far right." They even delude themselves into thinking the left—they—are always right and the "Right Is Wrong," as Arianna Huffington titled one of her silly books. The *Huffington Post* types dismiss conservatives as a "lunatic fringe" that threatens to "hijack" America.

Conservatives are neither to speak nor to be heard.

People hear the echoes of fake news when after a mass shooting the networks load up their guest lists for a "national conversation" in which there are nineteen voices demanding gun control for every defender of the Second Amendment. Or when the "LGBT" perspective is championed as news while anyone opposing it is a "born-again bigot" who doesn't deserve the time of day for his troglodyte "hate speech" rebuttal. Or when questioning the impending doom of "climate change"— or even questioning the cost of government efforts to "save us" from their hellish predictions—is treated like a "Flat Earth Society" viewpoint unworthy of public consideration.

The news product on television today is riddled with salesmanship. It is no longer journalism. These are campaign ads. In Democratic administrations, the advertisements are emphatically positive, like the arrival of a miracle stain remover or a wondrous kitchen gadget—*it slices, it dices, it makes julienne fries!* But when the Republicans win, reporters sound like negative campaign commercials in heavy rotation. *Mesothelioma kills you. Call this number to speak to our law firm.* You could detect their emotional undertone: These uneducated people and their dangerously simplistic patriotism and outdated moral values can't possibly represent a "mainstream" or a majority! In their Michael Moore mind meld, the liberal "majority" is being unjustly subjected to the elected "fringe" running the government. The inmates are in charge.

Under Trump, the news can feel like a never-ending tornado warning. It's designed to keep everyone perpetually uneasy. It sounds that the only way to get rid of the horror-movie echoes of the news is to get rid of the president.

These days we don't turn on the television and find a nightly "newscast." Instead, we are force-fed a nightly narrative. In the Trump era, that narrative insists that Trump is not just a bad president. He's so terrible that he needs to be removed from office immediately. Somehow, the most democratic outcome is for democracy to be overturned.

People think of that constant, lurid, aggravated noise when the president decries "fake news." And it resonates like no other issue in politics today.

The False or Fake News about Trump

Even by our more generous definition, the media have put out a massive pile of some seriously false news about Trump that they've been forced to correct. The public humiliation infuriates them, especially when they've had to demote or fire employees. Around the one-year anniversary of Trump's inauguration, someone in the Trump administration had a brilliant idea. The president proclaimed that he would cobble together a list of the worst fake news stories of 2017. The media went bonkers. The *New York Times* warned that the hubbub over a list "alarmed advocates of press freedom and heartened his political base." There you had it. On one side, the forces of freedom; on the other, supporters of Donald Trump.

The Media Research Center's blog site, NewsBusters, released its own list: the "Eight Times the Liberal Media Screwed Up on Trump-Russia in 2017." So many were fixated on Russia, putting the cart in front of the horse in trying to prove that Trump's election was imposed by Moscow. What about Hillary's connection to Russia (see the Uranium One deal)?

Here are the examples found in the report.

- CNN filed an explosive online report that claimed that the Senate Intelligence Committee was investigating the head of a massive Russian investment fund who met with Trump pal Anthony Scaramucci before Inauguration Day. The CNN story speculated that the two might have discussed the new administration lifting Russian sanctions—a tidbit that, if true, would have potentially big financial benefits to the investment fund.

The story cited only a single anonymous source, which showed how flimsy it was. And then it fell apart completely. By the next day, visitors to CNN's web page found a giant "Editor's Note" explaining that the story "did not meet CNN's editorial standards and has been retracted. . . . CNN apologizes to Mr. Scaramucci." The problem is that this story most certainly *did* meet their standards.

The three "investigative reporters" at CNN were fired.

- ABC's chief investigative reporter, Brian Ross, made the jaw-dropping claim that Trump's first (and quickly fired) national security advisor, Michael Flynn, would testify that during the 2016 campaign, then-candidate Donald Trump had "ordered him—directed him to make contact with the Russians, which contradicts all that Donald Trump has said to this point."

  If true, that conceivably would have put the president in legal jeopardy. Within minutes, Ross's report was being parroted across the national media, and the stock market fell more than 300 points. But it turned out that Ross had committed the biggest blunder of his career. Ross clarified hours later that Trump made the alleged request of Flynn not as a candidate but after he was elected—which made it a routine act of a transition team, not collusion.

  ABC put out a statement: "We deeply regret and apologize for the serious error we made yesterday. The reporting conveyed by Brian Ross during the special report had not been fully vetted through our editorial standards process." ABC suspended Ross for a month without pay and barred him from covering President Trump in the future. He later left ABC in disgrace.

- Trump's firing of FBI director James Comey (speaking of disgraces) was widely hyped as the opening scene of a new Watergate or worse. Previewing a congressional hearing that would star Comey, both ABC and CNN claimed that Comey would specifically dispute Trump's statement that he told the President "on three separate occasions, that I'm not under investigation."

   If this was true, Trump would have been lying about being a target of the investigation. Two days later, Comey said exactly the opposite, confirming that he had assured the President that he was not under investigation. Both CNN and ABC updated their web stories, but ABC never told viewers on television—that's where viewers had been misled—that its reporting was 100 percent fake news.

- A "bombshell" *New York Times* story had reported that "phone records and intercepted calls show that members of Donald J. Trump's 2016 presidential campaign and other Trump associates had repeated contacts with senior Russian intelligence officials in the year before the election" and particularly around the time of the e-mail hacking of the Democratic National Committee.

   If true, this wasn't contact just with Russians but with Russian spies. But as usual the *Times* had next to nothing but fog. Get a load of this sentence: "The officials would not disclose many details, including what was discussed

on the calls, the identity of the Russian intelligence officials who participated, and how many of Mr. Trump's
advisers were talking to the Russians."

In his Senate hearings, Senator Jim Risch (R–Idaho)
asked Comey directly about the *Times* story and whether
it was "a fair statement" to declare it was "not true."
Comey responded, "In the main, it was not true." He
added emphasis: "The challenge, and I'm not picking on
reporters, about writing on classified information is the
people talking about it often don't really know what's
going on, and those of us who actually know what's
going on are not talking about it. And we don't call the
press and say, 'Hey, you got that thing wrong.'"

Leakers may not be experts. Imagine that!

Yet the *New York Times* refused to withdraw its claim,
noting in its write-up only that "Mr. Comey did not say
exactly what he believed was incorrect about the article"
and that the paper's anonymous sources still stood by
their claims. "The original sources could not immediately be reached after Mr. Comey's remarks, but in the
months since the article was published, they have indi-
cated that they believed the account was solid."

This from the newspaper whose commercials during
the 2017 Oscars insisted "The truth is more important
than ever."

• CNN published an early-morning story claiming that
Trump, his son Donald Trump Jr., and other Trump
employees received an e-mail containing a "decryption

key and website address for hacked WikiLeaks documents" on September 4, 2016, nine days before they were publicly revealed on September 13.

If true, that would demonstrate a secret collusion between the campaign and WikiLeaks. Ooooops. Actually, the e-mail was dated ten days later, September 14, after the information was made available publicly.

But this was exposed only after CNN spent most of a day proudly touting a "BREAKING NEWS" banner and "CNN Exclusive" that claimed, "Emails Reveal Effort to Give Trump Campaign Wikileaks Documents." CNN had to announce an on-air correction but insisted that the cooks of this half-baked story had "followed the editorial standards process." Some process.

- Bloomberg News claimed that Special Counsel Robert Mueller had "issued a subpoena" to Deutsche Bank that "zeroed in" on President Trump personally. Their explosive headline: "Mueller Subpoenas Trump's Deutsche Bank Records, Source Says." After a cable-news frenzy over the mere thought of Mueller reaching into Trump's personal finances, Bloomberg had to backpedal, as the request was apparently not for the President's personal records but more vaguely for "documents and data related to people or entities affiliated with Trump."

- NBC News national correspondent Peter Alexander sent the media into a frenzy when he tweeted "BREAKING" news that the U.S. Treasury Department had announced it would, in his words, "allow some companies to do transactions with Russia's FSB, aka fmr [sic] KGB."

Alexander then phoned in to MSNBC, where the screaming headline claimed that the new administration was "easing U.S. sanctions on Russia."

Except that the sanctions weren't being eased. It was only a "technical fix, planned under Obama, to avoid any unintended consequences of cybersanctions," as an embarrassed Alexander noted in a follow-up tweet later in the day.

• Several media outlets made the outrageous claim that the "evidence" for Russian meddling in the election was the unanimous verdict of U.S. intelligence. "All 17 intelligence agencies have agreed Russia was behind the hack of Democratic email systems and tried to influence the 2016 election to benefit Trump," claimed one Associated Press report. That "17 intelligence agencies" line was repeated ad nauseam.

The AP and the *New York Times* eventually were forced to backpedal on those exaggerated claims, admitting that only three agencies (FBI, CIA, and NSA) had reviewed the intelligence, which was then issued by a fourth, the Office of the Director of National Intelligence. AP issued a correction that it had spread a false number in four separate articles: "Not all 17 intelligence agencies were involved in reaching the assessment." Interesting math, that. Less than one-quarter equals "not all."

Trump eventually left it to the Republican National Committee to post his list of the most flagrant fiascoes. They had plenty more to add to the bonfire of fake news:

- *Time* reporter Zeke Miller falsely tweeted that a bust of Martin Luther King Jr. had been removed from the Oval Office. It turns out Miller's view had been obscured by a door and a Secret Service agent. Nor did he ever bother to confirm the alleged absence of the MLK bust with anyone in the Trump administration. It was apparently "too good to check." Miller quickly apologized and said it shouldn't reflect on the magazine. Which of course it should.

- *Washington Post* political scribe Dave Weigel tweeted out a picture of an empty theater, mocking a rally in Pensacola as "packed to the rafters," but the picture was taken hours before the crowd arrived. He deleted it and apologized and said it shouldn't reflect on his newspaper. Which of course it did.

- *Newsweek* wrongly reported that Polish First Lady Agata Kornhauser-Duda did not shake President Trump's hand in Warsaw despite videotaped evidence to the contrary. They opted for this all-caps blaring headline: "WATCH DONALD TRUMP HANDSHAKE REJECTED BY POLISH FIRST LADY IN HILARIOUSLY AWKWARD EXCHANGE." The story began, "On Thursday, the world was once again blessed with an unusual, albeit hilarious, apparent slight, this time involving Trump and the first lady of Poland." There was no snub. The Polish first lady had passed by the president to shake hands with the American first lady—and then came right back to Trump.

- CNN deceptively edited a video to make it appear that President Trump bumbled into overfeeding fish during a visit with Japanese Prime Minister Shinzo Abe. "Trump Feeds Fish, Winds Up Pouring the Entire Box of Food into a Koi Pond," one CNN headline read, as if he had dumped it out of cultural ignorance. In the original video put out by CNN's Twitter account, the camera zoomed in tight on the President while he threw food to the fish with a spoon before he dumped his whole box into the water. What wasn't in CNN's video? The Japanese leader dumping his box of fish food first, before Trump followed.

Some of these "scoops" were tiny thimbles on a scale of newsworthiness but still were intended to keep the tone of Trump's news as negative as possible. Anywhere. Any time. And any way.

Former CBS News reporter Sharyl Attkisson made her own list of fifty-eight major media mistakes in the Trump era, and she explained how they often happen. Reporters claim that Trump statements are "lies" when they are matters of opinion or when the truth is unknowable because sources contradict one another. She documented how journalists report second-hand accounts of what Trump said or did without attribution as if this juicy gossip were established fact. Trump's statements are twisted out of context to underline an anti-Trump narrative that he's stupid or racist or mentally unfit.

"What's worse, we defend ourselves by trying to convince the public that our mistakes are actually a virtue because we (sometimes) correct them," Attkisson wrote. "Or we blame Trump for why we're getting so much wrong. It's a little bit like a police officer taking someone to jail for DUI, then driving home drunk himself: he may be correct to arrest the suspect, but he should certainly know better than to commit the same violation."

Journalists often insist that the mistakes constitute a small fraction of what they do. So why refuse to apologize or even just admit they messed up? Do you really demonstrate a great care for the facts by refusing to acknowledge error—any error?

You can hear journalists grinding their teeth at this discussion. *All you conservatives do is bitch about our mistakes, not the good work we do!*

The media wouldn't like to have this logic turned back around on them. They don't cover the airplanes landing on time; they cover the crashes. They don't cover the restaurants serving good food; they cover the restaurants that gave customers food poisoning. They don't cover the tens of millions—hundreds of millions?—of conservatives who despise racism; they cover the handful who support it. If you think focusing on media mistakes "undermines" the press, journalists should live up to their own message and stop focusing on every other industry or government agency that makes mistakes or every cause with a minuscule fringe that is truly deplorable and is rejected by the vast majority.

When the Trumped-Up "News" Thrives on Emotion

There's also tonality. So much of the biased news about President Trump is presented in emotional verbs and adjectives about a chief executive with an anger-management problem. Reporters seem incapable of describing events and debates and issues soberly as they unfold. During the eight years of his presidency, Barack Obama was routinely described as a cool customer, not easily flustered or made angry. There was no interest in palace intrigue. He didn't cause anxiety; he calmed it. In one story on Obama selling Obamacare, NBC's Mike Viqueira reported, "This week the president continued to try and calm public anxiety." He followed that with this now-infamous sound bite: "If you like your private health insurance plan, you can just keep it."

It's easy to be calm when you can lie through your teeth in order to confiscate one-seventh of the American economy—and no reporter will call you out on it.

When Obama sulked—which he did routinely if his demands were challenged—they would attribute it to the whole team, not to him. When Israeli prime minister Benjamin Netanyahu was invited to speak before Congress, NBC reported, "The White House and Democrats are fuming because they say the prime minister snubbed the President by accepting an invitation to address Congress from Republican House Speaker John Boehner without consulting the White House."

NBC preferred people to gush over Obama's temperament, as *Time* editor Richard Stengel did on *Meet the Press* in comparing Obama favorably to their South African icon Nelson Mandela in 2010: "Nelson Mandela went to prison when he was almost Barack Obama's age. He was there for 27 years. He was a hard-headed, tempestuous revolutionary who went into prison, and he came out as this calm, measured man." And here it came: "You know, Obama's temperament is kind of amazing. He sort of formed it without having to go to prison for 27 years, which I wouldn't wish on anybody. So there's some similarity there."

By contrast, network reporters seized on Trump's combative tweets or anonymous reports of Trump's alleged rages to paint Trump as emotionally unstable. NBC reporter Hallie Jackson relayed, "Multiple sources describe his mood as volcanic."

To test their use of subjective and emotional lingo, Media Research Center analysts looked at every broadcast evening news story about the President from January 1 through September 10, 2018, and tallied how many times the various words had been used by reporters to describe Trump's state of mind. The numbers were staggering.

Broadcast journalists were the most likely to describe the President as angry. ABC, CBS, and NBC described Trump as angry 185 times during the study period, or roughly 20 times per month.

They often used highly charged words to paint him as unhinged or out of control. Viewers heard Trump variously described as "furious" (seventeen times), "fuming" (fourteen), "outraged" (eight), "venting" (five), "infuriated" (five), "livid" (three), "enraged" (three), "seething" (two), or just plain-old "angry" (twenty-three).

When Trump communicated, he was said to be "lashing out" (fifty-three times), on a "tirade" (eight), "blasting" (five), or "erupting" (three). The President was also "on the warpath," "volcanic," "unglued," and "spoiling for a fight" and even "went ballistic," according to reporters at various times that year.

ABC's *World News Tonight* accounted for more than half of this language: 106 times. For example:

- David Wright told viewers: "President Trump [is] on the warpath, demanding answers about reports that the FBI had an informant approach the Trump campaign."

- After Canadian Prime Minister Justin Trudeau criticized Trump at the G-7 summit, ABC's Martha Raddatz declared that "the President went ballistic."

- A month later, ABC reporter Terry Moran said that Trump was "furious about a recent $12 billion gas pipeline deal Germany signed with the Kremlin."

- After an "anonymous" op-ed appeared in the *New York Times*, chief White House correspondent Jon Karl said the President was "enraged at the idea of an enemy within his own administration."

CBS's and NBC's reporters also attempted to psychoanalyze the commander in chief, just not as frequently. NBC's Hallie Jackson said the President "became unglued this week, in the words of one source," which left him "seething and spoiling for a fight."

Besides the various synonyms for anger, reporters described the President as "frustrated," "aggravated," or "dismayed" a total of thirty times, and viewers heard him called "worried," "anxious," "shaken," or "afraid" on fourteen occasions, outstripping the six instances when he was cast as "confident," "relieved," or "not worried."

In contrast, reporters described Trump's state of mind as happy a total of twenty-three times, using words such as "ecstatic," "delighted," "thrilled," and "gleeful." Once, NBC correspondent Geoff Bennett told viewers that "people close to the President describe his mood as calm," the *only* time the word "calm" was used by an evening news reporter to describe the president during the study period.

This matched an earlier search to see how often ABC used the term "Twitter tirade" to describe Trump's tweets. The search found that over a year, there were twenty-five uses on ABC's morning and evening news shows. Fifteen were uttered by reporters, and another ten were on screen. When the cast of the Broadway musical *Hamilton* obnoxiously denounced the Trump administration from the stage with Vice President Mike Pence in the audience, Trump shot back on Twitter. The on-screen message was "WILL TWITTER TIRADE CREATE POLITICAL BACKLASH?" ABC's Dan Harris was leery: "Whatever you think of what the cast of *Hamilton* said, how politically wise was it for the president-elect to take them on, given the lingering concerns about both his temperament and his tolerance?"

In his first year as president, ABC also advertised on screen about "TRUMP'S EASTER TWITTER TIRADE" and "TRUMP RINGS IN 2018 WITH TWITTER TIRADES." Interestingly, ABC not once found a Twitter tirade against the President. ABC didn't use that term when CNN host Reza Aslan launched a Twitter tirade against Trump, including this beauty after a terrorist attack in London: "This piece of shit is not just an embarrassment to America and a stain on the presidency. He's an embarrassment to humankind."

Does anyone think this coverage hasn't affected the public's perception of Trump? A Quinnipiac poll released on September 10, 2018, showed that 65 percent of voters thought the President was "not level-headed," compared with 30 percent who thought he was level-headed, and a 55 percent to 41 percent majority said that Trump "is not fit to serve as President." But his favorability rating with his base remained unchanged. His supporters were not buying this.

They knew that no matter what this man said or accomplished, it would be spun against him. They were right.

3

It All Sucks

COVERING POLITICS WITH A sense of fairness requires journalists to acknowledge that politicians, even the ones they despise, at some point, somewhere, on some matter, do *something* right. Not so with Donald Trump. Journalists simply cannot admit that anything Trump has done or is doing or is thinking of doing is good for the United States because it will reflect positively on him. That they just won't allow.

Since he announced his run for the presidency, Trump has drawn more negative press than any presidential candidate or President in history. President Trump's staunchest enemies—liberals and Never Trumpers alike—will argue that this is the truly objective, and fair, and accurate read on the present condition.

How they can say this with straight faces escapes us.

Month after month going back to the start of his campaign, without interruption, his coverage on evening newscasts has hovered around 90 percent negative. How do the anti-Trumpers see this? Some, such as Don Lemon, dismiss the numbers: "Is that a scientific mathematical fact, 90 percent?" Most don't care either way.

Trump haters will argue that even 90 percent negative coverage is too kind and demonstrates some sort of weakness, failing to provide the fullest measure of #Resistance. To acknowledge that Trump got two outstanding Supreme Court justices confirmed, or succeeded in passing a massive corporate tax bill that has generated massive employment numbers, or has taken millions off the welfare rolls, or virtually destroyed ISIS, or wiped out thousands of oppressive regulations, or—really, should we continue?—isn't providing news. It's enabling an oppressive fathead.

Every new and successful Trump policy concomitantly exposes the failures of his predecessor. Barack Obama can only watch in what should be shame as his policy prescriptions on the economy, on foreign policy, on regulation, and on pretty much everything else are proved to have been failures. But this man has no shame, and neither do his acolytes. Instead he hits the road giving his pathetic "Look at me! Look at me! I did it, yes I did!" speeches to steal the credit. And reporters trip over their own camera cords running to give him coverage.

Look at the spin of Trump's coverage on the ABC, CBS, and NBC evening newscasts since July 29, 2016, when the conventions ended, the candidates had been nominated, and the general election contest was officially running.

There were 95 positive statements about Trump. There were 726 negative ones. (That computes to 88 percent negative spin, Mr. Lemon.) Throughout the general election campaign the tone was remarkably steady: In August, the spin was 87 percent negative; in September, it was 94 percent negative; and in October, it was 90 percent negative. Statisticians call this the "mean" . . . and it was certainly mean.

Oh, but it gets better. Now look at the content flavoring the empirical data. Describing it as merely "negative" does not do it justice. "Donald Trump spoke off the cuff, and took his campaign off the rails," sputtered CBS anchor Scott Pelley to describe ignorant Trump. "Trump, diving head-first into the politics of fear," claimed NBC reporter Hallie Jackson to describe unethical Trump. His rallies were "swallowed by fear, anger, and misinformation." ABC's Tom Llamas quoted *New York Times* columnist Thomas Friedman on screen to describe Trump as a threat to humankind: "Trump knows what he's doing, and it is so dangerous in today's world!" (Llamas conveniently skipped the part in that column where Friedman suggested that Trump's tone would trigger an assassination.)

That was during the campaign. Now look at the numbers for President Trump, beginning on Inauguration Day, January 20, 2017. That is the initial one- to two-month stretch known traditionally as the "honeymoon" period in which the new President is given time to get his presidential sea legs.

Remember Obama's honeymoon period? It could not have started on a happier note.

ABC's Bill Weir oozed out that "never have so many people shivered so long with such joy. From above, even the seagulls must have been awed by the blanket of humanity." CNN anchor Carol Costello was thrilled: "It was a giant lovefest.... When Barack Obama started to speak, I was right in the middle of the crowd. People were crying, they were laughing, they were cheering. Suddenly someone would just come up and hug you. It was just amazing." NBC's Andrea Mitchell gushed, "What a day it was. It may take days or years to really absorb the significance of what happened to America today.... The mass flickering of cell phone cameras on the Mall seemed like stars shining back at him."

But for Trump? On his first night in office, the networks were brutal on his inaugural address. NBC's Chuck Todd denounced it: "I thought it was shockingly divisive for an inaugural. . . . He insulted—at points, insulted almost every living president that was there to witness his inaugural, which, to me, was so stunning!"

Over on ABC, Terry Moran was sniffing for hate when Trump used the term "America First," saying that "it carries with it overtones from the 1930s when an anti-Semitic movement saying, 'We don't want to get involved in Europe's war. It's the Jews' fault in Germany!' Charles Lindbergh led them. It is a term, as he defined it his way, but the words themselves carry very ugly echoes in our history."

New York Times correspondent David Sanger mourned that Trump could have somehow used the slogan "America First" in "the most inclusive way" but "instead, he chose a dark, hard-line alternative, one that appeared to herald the end of a 70-year American experiment to shape a world that would be eager to follow its lead."

There would be no honeymoon.

During the final twelve days of January, the traditional honeymoon spin was 85 percent negative, unheard of in modern politics. In both February and March, it hit 91 percent negative. In April, the President got a minimal surge of positive clips after he ordered a military strike against Syria for using chemical weapons on its own civilians. That generated a massive change in coverage. That month, the spin dove downward . . . to 82 percent negative.

It has been thus for every single month of Trump's presidency.

Just as with the campaign, the networks have centered their stories not on news but on that which the left has found the most objectionable about Trump. To the networks, the most urgent White House story was the attempt to impose a temporary ban on immigration from seven (and later six) Muslim countries. This issue was of minimum importance to the public, yet the coverage was massive and massively negative—93 percent. The second biggest story was their obsession over whether Russia "hacked the election" or improperly coordinated with Trump staffers, which to this day remains completely undocumented. That topic drew 97 percent negative coverage. Coming in third was the effort to repeal and replace Obamacare. That registered as 94 percent negative.

Trend, anyone?

They presented the new president as a terrible liar, and if not that, then potentially mentally ill. Three days after the inauguration, CBS's Pelley snapped that the president engaged in "a weekend of tweeting tantrums and falsehoods." On February 6, he knocked "presidential statements divorced from reality," and on March 8, he asked Democrat Leon Panetta: "Is it appropriate to ask whether the President is having difficulty with rationality?"

ABC's Moran felt bad for . . . European leaders. "He's been sent by the American people to change things. Right? And they're ready to do business with him. . . . And they're lost in the weeds of this adolescence out of Washington. . . . The White House, at this point, is a laughingstock in the capitals of Europe."

It wasn't any better on cable. Take Chris Matthews on MSNBC in March. "The man in the White House is demonstrably capable of making up claims that have no reality!" he yelped. "He's no better than the weirdo in the basement who calls in the fire alarm just to hear the sirens going past!"

The negativity was so inescapable that even liberal research outfits had to report it! The Pew Research Center looked at Trump's coverage during the first sixty days of his administration. According to Pew, that was "more than twice the negativity seen in stories from the first 60 days of Bill Clinton, George W. Bush or Barack Obama's presidencies." They had it at 62 percent negative, 5 percent positive, and 33 percent neutral. Interestingly, when you eliminate the neutral component, you get almost exactly the same ratio documented by the conservative Media Research Center: 92.5 percent negative.

Media scholar Thomas Patterson also studied the first 100 days of the Trump administration for the Shorenstein Center at Harvard's Kennedy School of Government. Yes, the

Harvard eggheads found the same reality. "Trump's coverage during his first 100 days set a new standard for negativity. Of news reports with a clear tone, negative reports outpaced positive ones by 80 percent to 20 percent," Patterson reported.

He continued: "Trump's coverage was unsparing. In no week did the coverage drop below 70 percent negative and it reached 90 percent negative at its peak. The best period for Trump was week 12 of his presidency, when he ordered a cruise missile strike on a Syrian airbase in retaliation for the Assad regime's use of nerve gas on civilians. That week, his coverage divided 70 percent negative to 30 percent positive."

More from Mr. Patterson: "Six of the seven U.S. outlets in our study—CBS, CNN, NBC, *The New York Times*, *The Wall Street Journal*, and *The Washington Post*—are among those he's attacked by name. All six portrayed Trump's first 100 days in highly unfavorable terms. CNN and NBC's coverage was the most unrelenting—negative stories about Trump outpaced positive ones by 13-to-1 on the two networks. Trump's coverage on CBS also exceeded the 90 percent mark. Trump's coverage exceeded the 80 percent level in the *New York Times* (87 percent negative) and the *Washington Post* (83 percent negative)."

Just as conservatives were saying. Just as *Trump* was saying!

All News Is Bad News

By spring, the Trump administration agenda was underway, and with lightning speed it was notching victories on both the domestic and the foreign policy fronts. But no matter what Trump accomplished—doesn't a booming economy count for *anything*?—the media onslaught continued.

The continuity was astonishing. From May through November 2017, every month was at least nine-tenths negative: 93 percent negative in May, 90 percent in June, 92 percent in July, 91 percent in August, 92 percent in September, 91 percent in October, and 91 percent in November.

The topics didn't matter. Whatever the issue, the tone was terrible. In May, June, and July, the top issue was Russia, Russia, and Russia. In August, pundits lashed out at Trump for his reaction to the rioting in Charlottesville.

In August, the networks pounded Trump for his tough rhetoric: "North Korea best not make any more threats to the United States. They will be met with fire and the fury like the world has never seen." In October, the Russia obsession was back. In November, they finally focused on tax cuts, but they are never fond of Republican tax cut plans. "Risky tax schemes," as Al Gore had lamented.

Finally, in December, the tone softened after the passage of those tax cuts combined with the attendant surge in the stock market. Eighty-five percent negative.

It is indisputable that no President in the history of the republic has been visited by such vitriol from the press. Yes, yes: some of the negative coverage was deserved. But no political observer this side of Maxine Waters can defend it as an exercise in fairness.

How Dare Your Government Cut Your Taxes!

As we said, the numbers, as wretched as they were, still don't tell the full story of the media's hostility to all things Trump.

On December 20, a delegation from Congress came to the White House to celebrate Trump's tax victory. Corporate tax rates, at 35 percent and the highest in the world, had been slashed to 21 percent, not nearly as low as the President and conservatives wanted but significant enough to break out the bubbly. Personal tax cuts, in contrast, were a mixed bag. They were time-limited until 2025 to meet congressional budget caps, and some middle-class taxpayers in high-tax blue states would see less of a cut after the removal of exemptions for state and local taxes.

That is not how the press viewed it, to put it mildly. As David Muir saw it on his ABC show, "The biggest tax cuts will go to the wealthy, [to] corporate America, and Republicans then argue that that money saved will then be reinvested in jobs and pay raises for the middle class. But will that happen? Not everyone is convinced, but the President is beaming."

"Not everyone," of course, was really the hardcore left— including Muir. Why not say so?

In a taped report, his colleague Cecilia Vega continued with that "but" theme. "The President calls the tax plan a middle-class miracle, designed to deliver tax cuts for all American families. But Corporate America gets a much bigger tax cut!" As the video portion ended and they were live once again, Muir wanted to know about "one other big question tonight, Cecilia. How much will this cost? Adding more than a trillion to the deficit. The President did not address this today."

Who was their source that stated it was a given, a matter of fact, that these tax cuts would cause a $1,000,000,000,000 deficit? "Nonpartisan congressional budget analysts."

Speaking of trillions, back in 2009, then-NBC host Matt Lauer had badgered GOP strategist Karl Rove over GOP opposition to Barack Obama's $1 trillion "stimulus package" vote. (Massive government deficit spending, good. Tax cuts, bad.) "If you add up the House and the Senate we have what, 219 Republicans? All but three of them voted against this plan," Lauer complained. "216 Republicans seem to have placed a bet on failure."

But when House Democrats *unanimously* voted no on the Trump tax cut, Lauer's colleague Lester Holt had no concerns that they had "placed a bet on failure." Instead he sounded like a DNC press release, complaining about the tax bill's alleged repeal of the individual mandate that required everyone to purchase insurance under Obamacare (which was never repealed, by the way). "Unable to repeal and replace Obamacare, Republicans are instead trying to undermine it. So is this a body blow to Obamacare?" NBC's Kasie Hunt saw potential doom for the GOP: "Republicans could already be paying a political price, with a new poll showing nearly half of Americans disapprove of the tax plan."

Could the media's negative spin have had something to do with it? When the Trump tax cut passed, Holt conceded, "Passing the sweeping tax cut is a critical win for the President and his party as they approach next year's midterm elections." But he still found a way to splash cold water on the GOP. "Their hope now: that the large number of Americans unhappy with the bill will learn to love it." Hallie Jackson used verbiage made famous by liberals to assault Reagan's tax cuts and added: "With its tax plan, the GOP is making a risky bet—that benefits to businesses will trickle down to everyone else." (Their own company, Comcast, handed out $1,000 bonuses to some employees.)

They've never reported that they were flat-out wrong. This was no "risky trickle." It was a serious plan based on sound, proven economics. And overnight it took off. Just months later there was record low unemployment for blacks, Latinos, and women.

The Immigration Story, Loaded with "Fear," "Dread," "'Terror," and Trump

Let's examine another issue that ignited a powerful national debate—and one in which once again the "news" media lined up unequivocally with the far left in opposition to the Trump administration.

Trump's message on immigration has been unmistakable from the start of his presidential campaign: Our borders are being overrun by illegal aliens, and that directly undermines the rule of law while wreaking havoc on the economy, not to mention allowing all manner of violent MS-13 gangbangers and lowlife rapists along with a dollop of worrisome Middle Easterners to sneak in. Build the wall.

The left-wing position: Open the borders to all.

The media took sides. In the first eighteen months of Trump's presidency, 92 percent of comments about his position on immigration were negative. The press accomplished this by carefully selecting who would be the focus of its "news" stories, starting with illegal immigrants and their families as well as banned travelers from selected Muslim countries along with their families. They were Trump's "victims."

Those groups, along with their lawyers, accounted for 478 of the 1,087 sound bites aired on those newscasts. An additional 163 sound bites came from protesters opposed to the administration's immigration policies. Then there were another 85 sound bites from activists associated with liberal groups such as the National Council of La Raza. Reporters rarely describe them as liberal groups, either. NBC simply called the NCLR "immigration advocates," not "amnesty for illegal immigration advocates."

Add them up: 726 statements against Trump and his policy.

What about the other side of the coin? Those newscasts aired eighty-three sound bites from law enforcement, thirteen from U.S. citizens identified as border residents (they managed to find three of those people who were opposed to Trump's policies!), and five from friends and family members of those who died because of crimes committed by illegal immigrants. There were only four sound bites from activists associated with groups committed to the enforcement of immigration laws.

That's about 102 sound bites, a disparity worse than 7 to 1.

Lopsided as it was, the networks' preference for sound bites from Trump's victims once again doesn't fully tell the story. It's the substance that's more shocking. Reporters and anchors made it a point to help amplify the messages of "fear," "panic," "dread," and even "terror" among those barred from entering the United States or facing deportation.

In February 2017, as Trump toughened enforcement on illegal immigration, NBC correspondent Gabe Gutierrez reported that "families of undocumented immigrants say they're now living in fear. . . . An immigration attorney in Atlanta says there is a sense of panic among her clients."

Weeks later, on *CBS Evening News*, Scott Pelley warned: "There is a growing sense of dread among immigrants in America."

Then in September 2017, the Trump team announced an end to Obama's executive order on "Deferred Action for Children Arrivals," which offered temporary amnesty for children of illegal aliens who were brought to America as children. ABC reporter Cecilia Vega highlighted how "dreamers like Jesus Contreras are terrified" before running a clip from Contreras himself. "I am disappointed that the President, as a man of God and as a man of faith, did not keep his word," he complained. "It's saddening. It's terrible."

On NBC, correspondent Jacob Soboroff profiled a "Dreamer" named Pablo Garcia who fretted that the decision was "just heartbreaking that, you know, I could be deported anytime . . . it's shocking." Over on CBS, anchor Anthony Mason mourned that "a promise kept by President Trump is a dream lost for thousands of undocumented immigrants."

"Undocumented immigrants," "Dreamers"—these are the words used by the left rather than saying what those people are: illegal aliens. In other words, shame on President Trump for upholding the rule of law—period.

The tone was similar in June 2018, when the topic became the "zero tolerance policy" that separated illegally immigrating parents from their children. Fill-in NBC anchor Blake McCoy reported that Trump's "hardline immigration policies are causing gut-wrenching pain for some families." Two days later, anchor Lester Holt defined the parameters as seen by his industry: "And now, the intersection where rigid government policy and human compassion collide, with the children of migrants at the center."

To enforce the law is rigid, to break it compassionate. Former NBC anchor Tom Brokaw said it all on *Morning Joe*: "For a long, long time, the Republican Party has been declaring war on Hispanics in this country."

Promoting Trash-Talking Books Now, How About Some Good Old-Fashioned Gossip?

There is no question that the early days of the Trump administration were marked by what appeared to be sheer chaos. The inmates were running the asylum, and White House chief of staff Reince Priebus could not control them. Senior policy advisor Stephen Miller, then–chief strategist Steve Bannon, counselor to the President Kellyanne Conway, legislative director Marc Short, communications director Sean Spicer, his successor Anthony Scaramucci, and Priebus himself—these were just some of Trump's staff members accused of kneecapping one another for political advantage on everything from titles to access to office space.

What was accurate and what was deliberate fabrication? Who knew? Who cared? This was too good to be true, even if it wasn't.

It became downright embarrassing by the time Axios reported that "White House leakers leak about leaking" and someone leaked to the *New York Post* that Trump was keeping a list of suspected White House leakers.

It was called a crisis when Michael Wolff's *Fire and Fury: Inside the Trump White House* unveiled a real source, Bannon, who mistakenly thought he was participating in (and hidden by) the usual not-for-attribution interview. He issued a whole series of insulting comments about Ivanka Trump ("dumb as a brick"); stated that the activities of Jared Kushner, Paul Manafort, and Donald Trump Jr. were "treasonous"; predicted that Donald Jr. would "crack like an egg on live television" because of special prosecutor Robert Mueller's investigation; and stated that Kushner was involved in money laundering.

How much of all these Wolff tales were true? Who knew? Who cared? Everything leaked by the proverbial anonymous sources was treated as newsworthy. The media were—and still are—positively giddy about each and every piece of uncorroborated gossip if it hurts this administration.

MSNBC host Andrea Mitchell asked Wolff, "What is the evidence, if any, that he [Trump] could be dyslexic, and because of his personality, is not willing to admit that?" She didn't even wait for an answer, jumping ahead to asking why the President can't just admit he's dyslexic the way Nelson Rockefeller did. On his show, Chris Matthews touted all Wolff's unproven gossip as superfactual. "We can argue around the edges, but the facts are like giant blocks of reality."

It was the first of several books in 2018 by a series of anti-Trump authors promoting all manner of wild slop.

Does anyone remember the networks delighting in gossipy books savaging Barack Obama or Bill and Hillary Clinton? Books such as Edward Klein's *The Amateur,* Dinesh D'Souza's *The Roots of Obama's Rage,* and Gary Byrne's *Crisis of Character* could hit or even top the best-seller list and were completely ignored by the "objective" media, which were loath to give any oxygen to an attack on their icons. But these days they fully participate in promoting anti-Trump tomes no matter how unproven the charges or discredited the authors.

Wolff had been granted a lot of access around the Trump administration, and whoever gave him that permission would soon regret it. Wolff reported that "senior White House officials" thought Trump was a "child," "a moron," and "an idiot."

Bingo! On NBC's *Today,* anchor Savannah Guthrie put him on the air, noting that Wolff claimed that "everyone around the President, senior advisers, family members, every single one of them questions his intelligence and fitness for office." Wolff eagerly doubled down: "Let me put a marker in the sand here—100 percent of the people around him!"

This was just silly. Would that include his son-in-law? His daughter? Both were and still are about as "around him" in the White House as you can get.

But rather quickly, the book began to fall apart. For example, the author claimed that Thomas Barrack Jr., a billionaire friend of Trump's, told a friend that Trump is "not only crazy, he's stupid." Barrack denied that he ever said such a thing. Katie Walsh, a former White House adviser, also disputed a comment attributed to her by Wolff: dealing with Trump was "like trying to figure out what a child wants."So what? MSNBC host Stephanie Ruhle dismissed concerns: "Even if not all of it is true, the spirit of the book is." NBC's Carol Lee invoked the Trump standard: "We should say NBC has not confirmed a number of the stories in this book—but broadly it fits with this narrative that we saw in the first year of the Trump administration, which was a lot of infighting and a lot of chaos and a lot of disorganization."

What she was actually saying was "The stories are unconfirmed, but what the hell. They sure fit our narrative."

But there's a difference between "infighting and chaos"—which was undeniably true with the Trump White House, at least in the beginning—and tall tales about White House staff unanimously calling the president "crazy" and unfit to serve.

The second "tell all" came in August from former White House aide (and for bona fides *Apprentice* contestant) Omarosa Manigault Newman, someone who dubiously, if not laughably, claimed to be positioned at the highest levels of the White House. In *Unhinged,* she claimed that a long-rumored tape of President Trump using the N-word on the set of *The Apprentice* actually exists. She wrote that her hunt for the tape was the reason for her unceremonious firing in December 2017 but then admitted that she had never actually heard the offending recording. Post-publication, she told a very different story. This time she said she had just personally listened to a tape after her book had gone to press. She produced White House conversations that she personally recorded, but still no N-word tape.

So here's a character who misleads about her access to the President and makes accusations of vile behavior that are based on a tape she's never heard or seen and later says she heard but cannot produce. Would you call her credible?

You betcha! In one weekend, the three networks provided ninety-three minutes of free publicity for Omarosa's claims, with NBC alone offering fifty-seven minutes. As with the *Access Hollywood* tape, NBC seemed to be doing penance for the sin of building Trump's national profile over the years with *The Apprentice* and then *Celebrity Apprentice* and was more than willing to listen as Omarosa spoke sweet nothings into its ear: "I was complicit with this White House deceiving this nation. They continue to deceive this nation [about] how mentally declined he is, how difficult it is for him to process complex information, how he is not engaged in some of the most important decisions that impact our country." No grudge there.

Instead of producing the evidence, Omarosa demanded that the media ask the president if he ever used the N-word. NBC's Kristen Welker obliged, yelling the question at Trump on the south lawn of the White House and then proclaiming, "Overnight, President Trump ignoring tough questions." Trump *had* denied ever using the word, but not to this obnoxious reporter.

The media enjoyed the infighting even as they dismissed both sides. *New York Times* reporter Nicholas Confessore announced on MSNBC that it was a "ridiculous sideshow," but it's like two villains at war: "it's like watching Darth Vader kill the Emperor in the third *Star Wars* movie."

In September, they finally had a "legend" to promote: the Man Who Brought Down Nixon. *CBS Evening News* anchor Jeff Glor announced, "The latest book on the Trump White House paints an ugly picture of the current presidency. Bob Woodward, whose reporting helped bring down President Richard Nixon, says Chief of Staff John Kelly said, 'We're in Crazy Town.'"

It was actually a lot worse than that. In Woodward's book *Fear,* Kelly is quoted as saying of Trump: "He's an idiot. It's pointless to try to convince him of anything. He's gone off the rails. We're in Crazy Town."

In a statement, Kelly flatly disputed maligning the president like that: "The idea I ever called the President an idiot is not true, in fact it's exactly the opposite." He added, "He and I both know this story is total BS."

The book also quotes Defense Secretary Jim Mattis as saying after a meeting with the president that Trump acted like and had the understanding of "a fifth or sixth-grader."

Mattis issued a statement, tweeted at least twice by Trump, saying, "The contemptuous words about the President attributed to me in Woodward's book were never uttered by me or in my presence." Mattis called the book "the product of someone's rich imagination."

At best this was secondhand information. But it could also be false information designed to inflict damage. So was all of it true? Any of it true? Who cares? Print it.

Woodward claimed that these men were liars and that his anonymously sourced mudslinging directed at the President from his top appointees was the truth. Other journalists accepted his claim that their denials were no more than "political statements to protect their jobs." Woodward insisted that publishing unrecorded insults that are flatly denied by those he alleges made them—and that they knew, had they made them, would thoroughly damage the presidency and could well get them dismissed and publicly humiliated—provides "one of the building blocks of good journalism and book writing."

Chris Matthews agreed and marveled over all three of these sleazy books full of unproven stories, comparing them to . . . the Bible? "At the risk of blasphemy, all these authors do have sort of a rhyming aspect to them like the synoptic gospels of Matthew, Mark, and Luke."

4

Good News Is No News

"GOOD NEWS IS NO news; bad news is great news." It's an old saying and applies to the entire news media, particularly television, with its ambulance-chasing video advantage. They all do it. "Just ahead: An armed robber meets a senior citizen who is also armed. You're not going to believe what happens next!" With that tease, viewers must suffer through endless commercials before they can see the five-second grainy surveillance footage from the convenience store camera showing Grandma capping the hooded gangbanger.

Meanwhile, North Korea has launched a nuclear warhead and it's headed for Seattle.

The flip side of the equation is what concerns us now. When good news is cast aside to make room for the sensational, how well is the public served by an industry that purports to bring its audience the news of the day? The answer is not well, of course. But what if that news is censored *because* it's good news?

In the case of Donald Trump, the media just aren't going report news as good news—period. It just doesn't matter how many successes he's racked up in only two years. The list is endless and awesome.

In October 2018, the White House released a list of 289 accomplishments in its first twenty months alone. Most victories had conservatives fist pumping while leftists and swamp monsters recoiled in horror. They deserved coverage, and if they were offset by the Democrats' opposition, that would be appropriate. Here's but a sampling (with the prerequisite spin removed where necessary).

- 3.9 million Americans off food stamps since the elections

- Twenty-two deregulatory actions for every new regulation

- Signed legislation to roll back costly and harmful provisions of Dodd–Frank

- Biggest corporate tax cuts and reforms in history

- Killing of Obamacare's individual mandate penalty tax

- Most U.S. Circuit Court judges confirmed in a president's first year in history

- Movement of the American embassy from Tel Aviv to Jerusalem

There are political considerations in that list, and liberals can have honest disagreements about the "accomplishments" notation.

However, there are some accomplishments on that list that only an anti-American could dispute as such. They not only were positive news for the country but were positive in a profound way. Republicans can only pray that Democrats will be foolish enough to challenge these as successes. To dispute them publicly would be political suicide. Look at just a handful of them among the dozens upon dozens that fall in this category:

- 4 million new jobs since the elections

- ISIS defeated militarily

- Poverty rates for blacks and Hispanics at the lowest levels ever recorded

- Arrests of 228 illegal aliens affiliated with MS-13

- Successful negotiation of a new historic United States–Mexico–Canada trade agreement

- Unemployment for women at the lowest level in 65 years

- ICE arrest of more than 127,000 illegal aliens with criminal convictions or charges

Most examples from the White House accomplishment list dealt with the economy, and for good reason: The Trump administration's economic policies have reversed the Obama malaise and shattered the idea of a flatlined economy as the new normal for this country.

The economy has been a central issue in campaigns since forever. "It's the economy, stupid." What constitutes success in economic matters is a matter of spin with the press, however. Liberal elites thought Obama's 1.9 percent growth was not just commendable but evidence that their economic calculations somehow were bearing fruit and said so with enthusiasm. They also were convinced that President Trump would destroy their economic nothingburger and said so in no uncertain terms. Economist Stephen Moore had a field day rounding up some of the more entertaining predictions that already looked very wrong at the end of year 1.

- A month before the election, a *Washington Post* staff editorial: "A President Trump could destroy the world economy." Trump's protectionist impulses "not only would undo the work of generations and lower the United States' standing among the nations; it also would license other nations to conduct themselves just as selfishly. The disruption to market confidence could breed economic damage in excess of any transitory benefits."

- On MSNBC's *Morning Joe*, economic guru Steve Rattner: "If the unlikely event happens and Trump wins you will see a market crash of historic proportions, I think. . . . The markets are terrified of him."

- From *Politico*: "Economists: A Trump win would tank the markets . . . financial markets strongly prefer a Hillary Clinton presidency."

- Dartmouth College economics genius Eric Zitzewitz: "You saw Clinton win the first debate and her odds jumped and stocks moved right along with it. Should Trump somehow manage to win you could see major Brexit-style selling."

- But our favorite prediction comes yet again from the gift that never ceases giving: *New York Times* columnist Paul Krugman. Has this man ever gotten anything right? How many times have we heard him predict the end of the world should a conservative even contemplate something—horrors—fiscally sound? He foresaw end times on election night: "It really does now look like President Donald J. Trump, and markets are plunging. When might we expect them to recover? If the question is when markets will recover, a first-pass answer is never." Good Lord, was this man depressed: "So we are very probably looking at a global recession, with no end in sight. I suppose we could get lucky somehow. But on economics, as on everything else, a terrible thing has just happened."

The Boston Globe despised the Trump agenda so ardently that on April 9, 2016, it published an entirely fake-news satirical front page dated one year later, imagining the nightmare of a President Trump. One fake story was headlined "U.S. Soldiers Refuse Orders to Kill ISIS Families." In another satirical story, Trump offended the Chinese first lady by naming his new dog after her. Another predicted, "Markets Sink as Trade War Looms." (The chart attached to it showed the Dow Jones at 9,912. On the actual date of April 9, 2017, it was almost a thousand points higher. Oops.)

No one in his right mind can deny that the economy has boomed since Trump took office. It's been profound. "It's the economy, stupid."Once upon a time that was considered indisputable truth. Let's take a look at how Trump's economy was covered by the networks.

The Bureau of Economic Analysis announced on October 26, 2018, that the economy grew by 3.5 percent in the third quarter. Compare that to the BEA number under Obama for the year 2016: 1.6 percent. To its credit, the *New York Times* reported that 3.5 percent was "keeping it on track for the best annual performance since 2005." Newsworthy? ABC, CBS, and NBC skipped this story entirely.

The three networks all noted the 2018 second-quarter growth of 4.1 percent (later revised upward to 4.2), but CBS found an economist who called it "a bit of a mirage." To be sure, the first quarter of 2018 showed only 2.3 percent growth, but it was clearly better than the "experts" had predicted. The networks took a pass on that.

The same thing has happened with positive employment/ unemployment news. On the first Friday of each month, the Bureau of Labor Statistics announces the number of jobs added to the economy and the unemployment rate. Had it been negative news, you can bet they would have covered it month after month. However, month after month the numbers only improved, but the good news was no news: The total combined evening-news coverage on those Fridays in 2017 was just over twenty minutes, or roughly sixty times less than than the time devoted to the Russian obsession.

Twenty-one months into the Trump era, unemployment dropped from 4.8 percent to 3.7 percent—the lowest rate since

December 1969. But it wasn't just the rate. The raw number of employed Americans reached records, repeatedly. In October 2018, it had hit more than 156.5 million. The economy added 434,000 manufacturing jobs in those months.

Better still, the historic employment trends spread across pretty much every demographic, with record-low unemployment for women, blacks, Latinos, Asians, and youth. Millennial snowflakes probably would quit their new jobs if they knew Trump was responsible for them. After all that talk about Trump being a threat to women, blacks, and Latinos, these economic reports showed otherwise.

That was in 2017. The trend continued in 2018, but Trump would be lucky if they stayed on an unemployment report for more than twenty seconds. On October 9, 2018, came the news that unemployment had dropped to the lowest levels in almost fifty years. The Big Three networks combined for exactly one minute of coverage. NBC gave it eighteen seconds . . . and then awarded over two minutes to—we're not making this up—the breaking "news" that *Saturday Night Live* cast member Kenan Thompson has been on the NBC show for sixteen years.

What about the stock market? It also took off like a rocket.

Thirty-one Dow records were set between January 1, 2017, and January 26, 2018. Those records included hitting 21,000, then 22,000, then 23,000, then 24,000, then 25,000, and finally 26,000. Overall, in 2017, the Dow Jones average rose more than 25 percent.

So the networks routinely ignored it.

Ah, but how they found it newsworthy when the market went down! On May 7, 2017, NBC's Lester Holt opened the show warning, "Market plunge! Jitters on Wall Street! Is the so-called Trump bump over?" He brought on MSNBC host Stephanie Ruhle to say that the good economy and Trump's agenda were kaput. "Think about the Trump rally. This was based on President Trump's pro-business policy promises—tax reform, infrastructure spending, deregulation. And where are they? They're hanging in the back. Right now all focus is on Russia. As you said, the special prosecutor has been named. We're not talking about that agenda anymore." But that was because his network and its allies on the others had deliberately chosen to take that course!

In January 2018, the President tried to prod them with a tweet: "Dow goes from 18,589 on November 9, 2016, to 25,075 today, for a new all-time record. Jumped 1000 points in last 5 weeks, Record fastest 1000-point move in history." Still they yawned their lack of interest.

CBS briefly conceded, "This is now the second longest bull market on record," and moved on. NBC's Jo Ling Kent reported the news, noting that the markets liked the Trump tax cut, but found a way to give it a negative spin: "The stock market doesn't tell the whole economic story. Only half of American households own stock." A man on street added, "I think it's the people that are driving the economy. I don't think it's as much of the political game as they like to take credit for."

ABC reported absolutely *nothing* on the stock-market record. Instead, anchor David Muir was touting Michael Wolff's trashy book: "Steve Bannon turning on the President and his family, saying Don Jr.'s meeting in Trump Tower was treasonous." On the next night, David Wright had a whole story on Russia and the Wolff book—and then quoted Trump (talking about the market being "up very, very big") as trying to change the subject from what really mattered.

Russia speculation was "news." Actual financial facts were a distraction.

Throughout 2018 it was wash, rinse, and repeat. The networks continued to jump on losses and pass on gains. The network shows pounced on the "major selloff" and "meltdown" on October 10 and 11. One week before the Dow had set an all-time record high—the fifteenth record high of 2018. The Dow closed at 26,828.39 after rising five sessions in a row. They all skipped it.

So what about deregulation? Obama had starved small business by choking it to death with regulations. According to the Heritage Foundation, the regulatory frenzy of the Obama administration totaled "more than 23,000 regulations, including 285 major rules with $122 billion in cumulative annual costs" to the private sector economy.

Candidate Trump pledged to take this control away from useless government bureaucrats and restore the power of the free enterprise system. President Trump delivered, killing them by the thousands, and it worked just as he'd advertised. In a September 2017 editorial, *Investor's Business Daily* praised Trump's actions, saying that the deregulatory actions "will pay economic dividends for years to come."

Yet the Big Three networks were evidently unimpressed, or, like the leftists they are, they support big government, and so they gave the administration's push to deregulate barely eleven minutes of evening news coverage for the entire year. That's less than 0.2 percent of their total coverage of the administration. The patterns continued in 2018: Good news was no news.

Remember all that talk about how the United States would always be dependent on Saudi Arabia and other OPEC dictatorships for its energy? Obama's policies kept America subservient. He dragged his feet on any new pipelines to please his leftist environmental anti-fossil fuel base. Candidate Trump promised to put an end to that nonsense.

Soon after taking office, President Trump issued executive orders to expedite the building of two important pipeline projects that Obama wanted killed: the Keystone XL pipeline and the Dakota Access pipeline. In a January 2018 editorial, the *National Review*—a publication that had staunchly opposed Trump during the GOP primaries—praised the move. "Moving forward on these and other projects means work and wages for those who build them and for those who work at the facilities on both ends of the pipelines," wrote the editors. "It also means more abundant and more economical fuel, feed stock, and raw materials for industrial concerns at home and abroad, from plastics plants in China to chemical producers in Texas."

Reporters lauded Obama's antipipeline efforts, but Trump's deregulation? It earned him just over seven minutes from the ABC, CBS, and NBC evening newscasts in 2017, or roughly 0.1 percent of the networks' total Trump coverage. They offered exactly zero coverage of pipeline policies in the first nine months of 2018.

Let's continue. During the Obama administration, the networks put the national spotlight on the scandal at the U.S. Department of Veterans Affairs, ABC anchor Diane Sawyer correctly called it a "national outrage" that some veterans were dying while on waiting lists for proper care.

In every rally, candidate Trump promised to put an end to this disgrace. In 2017, President Trump delivered. In June, the President signed a bill that enabled top VA officials to fire incompetent workers and protect whistle-blowers. In August he signed a bill extending another $2 billion in funding to the Veterans Choice Act, a bipartisan measure allowing veterans to seek care outside the VA system if they need it. (Imagine that.)

But the networks' interest in telling viewers about these reforms was practically nonexistent. Out of 5,943 minutes of coverage of the Trump administration in 2017 the VA got exactly 3 minutes and 32 seconds. In the first nine months of 2018, the media added only another 3 minutes and 4 seconds.

After the economy, Trump's biggest accomplishments came in Supreme Court nominations.

President Trump's choice of Judge Neil Gorsuch to serve on the U.S. Supreme Court received reasonable coverage, mostly political analysis of the confirmation. Then came Brett Kavanaugh, and the coverage exploded.

Clarence Thomas, call your office.

It was as dishonest as it was coordinated, one of the most despicable assaults on a man's dignity this country has ever witnessed, a campaign of character assassination designed to derail his nomination to the court and defended as such by those who engaged in it! A good man's innocent wife was publicly humiliated, and his little girls tormented. Imagine being a child who has to listen to her dad being called a rapist on national television.

The national news media gave it all national coverage, one disgusting day after the next.

In the first twelve days after Democrats unfurled the unproven accusations of Christine Blasey Ford, the ABC, CBS, and NBC evening and morning shows spent nearly six hours regurgitating those horrific smears of sexual harassment (and worse) allegations against the Supreme Court nominee. Only a tiny percentage of that coverage—a measly 8 percent—was devoted to Kavanaugh's denials or focused on how the allegations were uncorroborated!

Trump's foreign policy achievements also were ignored. They loved Obama's policies and priorities, from ISIS to the Paris climate treaty to the Iran nuclear deal. And his style as he crisscrossed the globe apologizing for American exceptionalism? They were so excited, they levitated.

But then Trump came along and screwed it all up.

Obama drew no harsh coverage from the networks in 2014 when he dismissed the rise of ISIS in a basketball metaphor as a "JV team," even when those alleged amateurs took control of an area the size of Indiana, the largest terrorist sanctuary in history, using some of the most violent and extreme forms of terrorism in history. Decapitations, burnings, crucifixions— these were but some of the methods those monsters employed to punish their victims and scoff at Obama's JV designation.

That "caliphate" completely collapsed under Trump when he let General Mattis & Co. tear the ISIS army apart piece by piece. When they lost their home base in Raqqa in October 2017, the caliphate was no more. Coalition forces had regained nearly all the territory those savages had occupied in 2015 with Obama in power with Kerry as his secretary of state.

The President and his administration have received virtually no credit for this achievement. From Inauguration Day through September 2018, the three broadcast network evening newscasts offered more than 10,000 minutes of coverage of the Trump presidency. Winning the war against ISIS in Iraq and Syria drew only 33 minutes of attention—a *third of 1 percent* of the Trump total.

Though reporters spent little time discussing the President's military successes against ISIS, they certainly were aware of them. NBC Pentagon correspondent Hans Nichols acknowledged as much in a rare *Nightly News* segment on December 31, 2017: "Since President Trump took office ISIS has lost some 15,000 square miles to local forces with support from U.S. air power. The number of ISIS fighters is down from 35,000 to around 1,000. In Iraq and Syria, President Trump's strategy is similar to his predecessors' but his commanders on the ground have more authority."

When (your taxes-funded) National Public Radio asked leftist Vox.com editor Matthew Yglesias for "one overlooked political story of the year," even he admitted, "I think the sort of success of the American military campaign against ISIS has gotten remarkably little attention if you think about how alarmed people were a few years ago and how much it's really faded."

Not that NPR was any better. They too tried repeatedly to spin this against the administration. Do a quick search of the NPR archives and you'll find headlines hunting for a gloomy echo: "Thousands More Civilians Than ISIS Fighters Are Believed Killed in Mosul Battle," "Pentagon Says It's Staying in Syria, Even Though ISIS Appears Defeated," "With Mattis

Trip to Philippines, Reminders of Waning U.S. Influence in Region."

What About Positive Press for the Trumps Abroad?

When Obama wasn't using Air Force One for his endless vacations (including transporting his dog Bo in a separate plane with staff from Washington to Maine), he was globe-trotting. How the media loved it. Sure, he was the first black man to represent the United States. Yes, some of the crowds were enormous. And it's undeniable he knows how to use a teleprompter like no other.

When Barack and Michelle Obama flew to London in 2009, the gush was off the charts. First came the inevitable Kennedy comparisons, such as the one from NBC reporter Keith Miller: "What the Obamas bring to Buckingham Palace is a charisma not seen since the Kennedys, when the First Lady, Jacqueline, dazzled the royal court."

He wasn't the only one to wet his pants. NBC anchorman Brian Williams oozed, "There is no denying the Obamas from America are receiving a rock star reception on this trip. One London paper today called them American royalty." NBC White House correspondent Chuck Todd caught the fever too: "America's unofficial royalty, the President and First Lady, reconnected tonight for more ceremonial duties, including a private audience with actual royalty, the Queen herself."

Over on CNN, reporter Alina Cho chucked aside the qualifier altogether: "As America's First Lady embarks upon her first trip to Europe, the world is watching the royal family of the United States."

Now compare this with Trump's visit to London in June 2018. The press delighted in the thousands of (leftist) protesters. "Breaking overnight, not-so-royal welcome," proclaimed co-host Hoda Kotb at the top of NBC's *Today Show*. "Massive protests greet President Trump in London as he meets the British Prime Minister and the Queen today." For good measure they added a clip of protesters booing the president.

NBC's Richard Engel offered the classic media shtick. A raging crowd of left-wing protesters is always called a "diverse" gathering. "I am in central London right now, there are thousands of people here and there will be tens of thousands in central London as the day progresses. This is a very diverse crowd—men, women, old, young, straight, LGBT— there is an ethnically diverse crowd here. But they all have one message, they say that President Donald Trump is not welcome in this city."

The civilized world versus Donald Trump.

CBS White House correspondent Weijia Jiang touted how Sadiq Khan, the leftist Muslim mayor of London, was giving "protesters permission to fly this 20-foot balloon over Parliament today, depicting Mr. Trump as an angry baby." No one in the press seemed fazed in the least.

Leading off ABC's *Good Morning America,* co-host Robin Roberts told viewers, "President Trump saying he feels unwelcome in London this morning, responding to that 20-foot baby blimp as protesters fill the streets." Minutes later, correspondent Terry Moran repeated the report: "And as protesters against the president gathered on the streets of London, Trump says he feels unwelcome. Singling out the Trump baby blimp that will be flying all day."

Oh, how those impartial observers were enjoying this Trump-baby stuff! MSNBC host Ari Melber interviewed Asad Rehman of the protesting group War on Want. He should have confronted him for insulting a U.S. President. He didn't, of course. "The President, very sensitive about the idea that he's a baby—where does that fit into these protests?" Rehman replied, "Well, we know that the President is notoriously thin-skinned and a narcissist. I'm sure it will get under his skin." Melber, barely suppressing a smile, added drily, "Babies, also known for their thin skin."

Now wait a minute! the press will scream if Trump's supporters protest the coverage. *It happened. How can you deny its newsworthiness!*

Let's put aside the oxygen they fed into the story by showing such solidarity with the radicals. Let's concede their point and ask a question of our own: If the opposite occurred on a state visit, with Trump given a hero's welcome, would you cover it as such?

On July 6, 2017, President Donald Trump visited Warsaw, Poland. He was greeted by a huge cheering crowd in Krasinski Square and proceeded to deliver the most powerful speech of his presidency. We're not privy to the historical record, but we will go so far as to state that this certainly had to be the most profound address in his life, the words every bit as significant (if not eloquent) as anything prepared for Ronald Reagan. He was interrupted an endless number of times by an audience that roared its approval and appreciation.

It was an unequivocal celebration not just of Poland, not just of the United States, but of Western civilization itself.

Poland is the geographic heart of Europe, but more importantly, in the Polish people, we see the soul of Europe. Your nation is great because your spirit is great and your spirit is strong.

For two centuries, Poland suffered constant and brutal attacks. But while Poland could be invaded and occupied, and its borders even erased from the map, it could never be erased from history or from your hearts. In those dark days, you have lost your land but you never lost your pride. . . .

Despite every effort to transform you, oppress you, or destroy you, you endured and overcame. You are the proud nation of Copernicus—Chopin, Saint John Paul II. Poland is a land of great heroes. And you are a people who know the true value of what you defend. . . .

For Americans, Poland has been a symbol of hope since the beginning of our nation. Polish heroes and American patriots fought side by side in our War of Independence and in many wars that followed. Our soldiers still serve together today in Afghanistan and Iraq, combatting the enemies of all civilization. . . .

Our two countries share a special bond forged by unique histories and national characters. It's a fellowship that exists only among people who have fought and bled and died for freedom.

The signs of this friendship stand in our nation's capital. Just steps from the White House, we've raised statues of men with names like Pułaski and Kościuszko. The same is true in Warsaw, where street signs carry the name of George Washington, and a monument stands to one of the world's greatest heroes, Ronald Reagan.

And so I am here today not just to visit an old ally, but to hold it up as an example for others who seek freedom and who wish to summon the courage and the will to defend our civilization. The story of Poland is the story of a people who have never lost hope, who have never been broken, and who have never, ever forgotten who they are. . . .

In 1920, in the Miracle of Vistula, Poland stopped the Soviet army bent on European conquest. Then, 19 years later in 1939, you were invaded yet again, this time by Nazi Germany from the west and the Soviet Union from the east. That's trouble. That's tough.

Under a double occupation the Polish people endured evils beyond description: The Katyn Forest massacre, the occupations, the Holocaust, the Warsaw Ghetto and the Warsaw Ghetto Uprising, the destruction of this beautiful capital city, and the deaths of nearly one in five Polish people. A vibrant Jewish population—the largest in Europe—was reduced to almost nothing after the Nazis systematically murdered millions of Poland's Jewish citizens, along with countless others, during that brutal occupation.

In the summer of 1944, the Nazi and Soviet armies were preparing for a terrible and bloody battle right here in Warsaw. Amid that hell on earth, the citizens of Poland rose up to defend their homeland. . . .

From the other side of the river, the Soviet armed forces stopped and waited. They watched as the Nazis ruthlessly destroyed the city, viciously murdering men, women, and children. They tried to destroy this nation forever by shattering its will to survive.

But there is a courage and a strength deep in the Polish character that no one could destroy. The Polish martyr, Bishop Mchał Kozal, said it well: "More horrifying than a defeat of arms is a collapse of the human spirit."

Through four decades of communist rule, Poland and the other captive nations of Europe endured a brutal campaign to demolish freedom, your faith, your laws, your history, your identity—indeed the very essence of your culture and your humanity. Yet, through it all, you never lost that spirit. Your oppressors tried to break you, but Poland could not be broken.

And when the day came on June 2nd, 1979, and one million Poles gathered around Victory Square for their very first mass with their Polish Pope, that day, every communist in Warsaw must have known that their oppressive system would soon come crashing down. They must have known it at the exact moment during Pope John Paul II's sermon when a million Polish men, women, and children suddenly raised their voices in a single prayer. A million Polish people did not ask for wealth. They did not ask for privilege. Instead, one million Poles sang three simple words: "We Want God.". . .

As I stand here today before this incredible crowd, this faithful nation, we can still hear those voices that echo through history. Their message is as true today as ever. The people of Poland, the people of America, and the people of Europe still cry out "We want God."

Together, with Pope John Paul II, the Poles reasserted their identity as a nation devoted to God. And with that powerful declaration of who you are, you came to understand what to do and how to live. You stood in solidarity against oppression, against a lawless secret police, against a cruel and wicked system that impoverished your cities and your souls. And you won. Poland prevailed. Poland will always prevail. . . .

A strong Poland is a blessing to the nations of Europe, and they know that. A strong Europe is a blessing to the West and to the world. . . . This continent no longer confronts the specter of communism. But today we're in the West, and we have to say there are dire threats to our security and to our way of life. . . .

We are confronted by another oppressive ideology—one that seeks to export terrorism and extremism all around the globe. . . .

During a historic gathering in Saudi Arabia, I called on the leaders of more than 50 Muslim nations to join together to drive out this menace which threatens all of humanity. We must stand united against these shared enemies to strip them of their territory and their funding, and their networks, and any form of ideological support that they may have. . . .

Today, the West is also confronted by the powers that seek to test our will, undermine our confidence, and challenge our interests. . . . We urge Russia to cease its destabilizing activities in Ukraine and elsewhere, and its support for hostile regimes—including Syria and Iran—and to instead join the community of responsible nations in our fight against common enemies and in defense of civilization itself.

Americans, Poles, and the nations of Europe value individual freedom and sovereignty. We must work together to confront forces, whether they come from inside or out, from the South or the East, that threaten over time to undermine these values and to erase the bonds of culture, faith and tradition that make us who we are. If left unchecked, these forces will undermine our courage, sap our spirit, and weaken our will to defend ourselves and our societies.

But just as our adversaries and enemies of the past learned here in Poland, we know that these forces, too, are doomed to fail if we want them to fail. . . . They are doomed not only because our alliance is strong, our countries are resilient, and our power is unmatched. . . . Our adversaries, however, are doomed because we will never forget who we are. . . .

We write symphonies. We pursue innovation. We celebrate our ancient heroes, embrace our timeless traditions and customs, and always seek to explore and discover brand-new frontiers.

We reward brilliance. We strive for excellence, and cherish inspiring works of art that honor God. We treasure the rule of law and protect the right to free speech and free expression.

We empower women as pillars of our society and of our success. We put faith and family, not government and bureaucracy, at the center of our lives. And we debate everything. We challenge everything. We seek to know everything so that we can better know ourselves.

And above all, we value the dignity of every human life, protect the rights of every person, and share the hope of every soul to live in freedom. That is who we are. Those are the priceless ties that bind us together as nations, as allies, and as a civilization. . . .

The memories of those who perished in the Warsaw Uprising cry out across the decades, and few are clearer than the memories of those who died to build and defend the

Jerusalem Avenue crossing. Those heroes remind us that the West was saved with the blood of patriots; that each generation must rise up and play their part in its defense and that every foot of ground, and every last inch of civilization, is worth defending with your life.

Our own fight for the West does not begin on the battlefield—it begins with our minds, our wills, and our souls. . . . Our freedom, our civilization, and our survival depend on these bonds of history, culture, and memory. . . .

Just as Poland could not be broken, I declare today for the world to hear that the West will never, ever be broken. Our values will prevail. Our people will thrive. And our civilization will triumph.

There was no live coverage. Indeed, the networks glossed over all of that within seconds. Minutes after ABC's Cecilia Vega said, "This is a packed crowd out here, and they were cheering on the president as he laid out the future in very stark terms," there came the turn: "But really it is that press conference that he held before taking the stage here that is making headlines this morning. President Trump was directly asked if once and for all he would definitively say that Russia did interfere with our election. He hedged. He didn't answer directly."

NBC's Hallie Jackson also quickly turned away. "That nationalistic speech, warmly received in Warsaw, is part of an overseas trip that so far has become a tale of two Trumps. On one hand, the President talking tough on Russia. . . . On the other, declining to say for sure Moscow meddled with our election even in the face of overwhelming consensus from the U.S. intelligence community."

And that was pretty much it.

Good news is no news.

5

Dying in Darkness

THE NATION'S TOP TWO newspapers responded to Donald Trump's election with arrogant new slogans, virtually declaring war on him. The *New York Times* aired TV ads proclaiming "Truth: It's more important now than ever." Apparently truth hadn't been *that* important when Barack Obama or Bill Clinton was President. The *Times* also sold T-shirts with that slogan, pairing with a Japanese fashion company, and sold them for $300, a pretty funny way to fight red-state Make America Great Again populism.

The *Washington Post* chose a new motto that is now published on its masthead every morning: "Democracy Dies in Darkness." Look out! Trump was going tyrannical, and by God, the *Washington Post* was going to stop that.

"This is actually something we've said internally for a long time in speaking about our mission," Shani George, communications director at the *Post*, told the *Huffington Post*. "We thought it would be a good, concise value statement that conveys who we are to the many millions of readers who have come to us for the first time over the last year."

Hollywood rushed to provide air cover for this new ground assault, fiercely lionizing the *Washington Post* as the defenders of peace and truth, or something. Steven Spielberg rushed to make his movie *The Post*, glorifying the paper and its owner Katharine Graham for suing the Nixon administration in 1971 over the "Pentagon Papers" on the Vietnam War. Meryl Streep was cast as the liberal matriarch in *The Post*, taking on malignant Richard Nixon, and the Hollywood left swooned in self-importance.

"The level of urgency to make the movie was because of the current climate of this administration, bombarding the press and labelling the truth as fake if it suited them," Spielberg explained to the British socialist newspaper *The Guardian*. "I deeply resented the hashtag 'alternative facts,' because I'm a believer in only one truth, which is the objective truth."

Josh Singer, who Spielberg brought in to work over the script, added, "What became clear while we were making this movie is the current threat against good institutional journalism." Just as Hollywood rushed to lionize *The Post*, other media outlets charged into the fray to laud Spielberg and Co.

It was an orgy of love. The *New York Times* played with *The Post*'s new Trump-era motto, titling its movie review "In *The Post*, Democracy Survives the Darkness." *Time* magazine called it "a superhero movie for real grown-ups." There was a rave review by the movie critic Ann Hornaday headlined "In 'The Post'," Streep and Hanks Lead a Stirring Homage to the Pursuit of Truth."

She's the movie critic for the Washington Post.

But is the media's goal always simply the "truth"? Didn't pretty much everyone at the Post want Nixon to lose to Hubert Humphrey and George McGovern? Wasn't Walter Cronkite seeking to end the Vietnam War while seeking "truth"? (After he retired, he finally admitted it.) Is "the truth" the only thing that matters to the climate change crowd at CNN? Is "the truth" what motivates reporters covering caravans? Was it "the truth" they were after during the Kavanaugh hearings?

Is "the truth" all that matters with Donald Trump?

They all described Trump as waging a "war on the press" and then denied they were involved. "We're not at war with the administration," proclaimed Marty Baron, the Washington Post's editor. "We're at work."

That's not the truth. "Democracy Dies in Darkness" is a call to war.

To underline the chumminess between the New York Times and the Washington Post in the Trump era, the Times published a story that attempted to shame Trump's attack on the "Amazon Washington Post." Media reporter Sydney Ember included a bucket of defensive quotes from Baron, saying he would not be "cowed" by the president's invective. "We cover him the way that we feel any president should be covered," he lied.

This is the newspaper that ran front-page Obama stories featuring quotes like this one from reporter Eli Saslow that read like soft-core porn: "The sun glinted off his chiseled pectorals sculpted during four weightlifting sessions each week."

Days later, *Vanity Fair* magazine published a story on internal squabbling between the left and the radical left inside the *New York Times* that included a funny line from managing editor Joe Kahn. Remarkably, it's even funnier than Baron's. "We consider it crucial to our future that we do not become an opposition-news organization," he explained. "We do not see ourselves, and we do not wish to be seen, as partisan media."

How clueless does that sound? In context, Kahn was simply talking about preserving whatever shred of an appearance of nonpartisanship his paper could retain, since pretending to be nonpartisan, no matter how ludicrous it sounds to conservatives, might give their Trump-bashing efforts more weight.

But no one, regardless of ideology, is going to buy that garbage. As a tweet, it was simply hilarious on its face.

In 2016, Baron pitched a fit when the Trump campaign temporarily withdrew press credentials from the *Washington Post*. This didn't mean they couldn't cover Trump. It just meant that *Post* reporters couldn't travel on the campaign plane. The *Post*'s editorial board harrumphed that "Mr. Trump capped a day of assaulting fundamental liberal democratic values by announcing he would ban Post reporters from covering his campaign events. If this is his inclination now, imagine how he might wield the powers of the presidency."

Holy smokes. The *Post* is that essential to the republic?

That was hypocritical, and they knew it. The *Post* didn't write an outraged editorial in 2015 when the Hillary Clinton campaign banned right-leaning reporter David Martosko of the London *Daily Mail* from her campaign print pool. They expressed no editorial-page outrage as the Obama administration routinely insulted and avoided Fox News, describing it as "not a news organization."

There was no editorial when days before the 2008 election the Obama campaign kicked three McCain-endorsing papers off its plane—the *Washington Times,* the *New York Post,* and the *Dallas Morning News*—to make room for the more enthusiastic Obama-promoting black magazines *Ebony, Essence,* and *Jet.* The *Post* did a brief news item headlined "Reporter Off Obama Plane: *Times* Editor Squawks."

It is the right of candidates and presidents.

But when Trump did the exact same thing, there was outrage. *This will not stand!* "Donald Trump's decision to revoke *The Washington Post's* press credentials is nothing less than a repudiation of the role of a free and independent press!" huffed Baron.

We embrace the notion of freedom of the press as a hallowed institution essential to the democratic process that provides the system of government with checks and balances. But no such honor exists in the industry today. There is no system of checks or balances when the Democrats are in charge, and their idea of "balancing" Republican power is to savage it mercilessly. Nobody makes a movie about old media warhorses fiercely and aggressively questioning Bill Clinton or Barack Obama. Among other reasons, the material for such a film is nonexistent. It would be true fiction.

Underneath all their "war on the press" outrage, the media are suggesting that no one has the right to check or balance *them.* To resist the "Resistance" is somehow undemocratic. They paint themselves as dangerously "under siege" when their political agenda is exposed and their commitment to "the truth" is questioned. Despite the superhero treatment of the *Post* at the Cineplex, journalists are not a more noble and conscientious species. They deserve ridicule.

Donald Trump mocks them mercilessly as fake-news factories, and they're horrified that anyone would dare treat them so. In their minds (and out of their mouths), America has entered an "authoritarian" phase and the ignorant deplorables just don't see it. But chanting "CNN sucks" at a rally is a rigorous exercise of freedom of speech even if it's coarse. It is not a repeal of the concept; it's a rejection of an industry that wraps itself around that concept as a means of advancing a far-left narrative.

During the Trump transition, CNN's resident media expert Brian Stelter attacked Trump's attempt to "delegitimize" the press, to somehow "create the idea that someone out there is the enemy." He wanted reporters to say the A-word: "I talk to international correspondents who say to you, 'This is exactly what authoritarians do. This is what strongmen do. This is what happens in authoritarian regimes.' I think we need to start using those words on TV, at least, to discuss the possibilities before us."

In the middle of the Brett Kavanaugh fight, Stelter appeared on a press panel discussion in Washington and admitted that this cavalcade of panic was overwrought. "I think some of the greatest fears of the Trump era have not come to pass. He has not kicked reporters out of the White House. We have not seen mass jailings of journalists. These were true fears after election night in 2016, given the president's awful rhetoric toward the press."

Translation: I panicked like a little girl. Sorry.

It's also been a regular trope of Stelter & Co. that Trump's "awful rhetoric" would put reporters in danger. "When we see people booing journalists at rallies, when we see the death threats that come in over social media, it's all part of this hate movement," Stelter argued. He didn't see his own hypocrisy. When a deranged man—who had no political motivation—shot and killed five employees at the Annapolis *Capital Gazette*, Stelter turned the beam toward Trump. "There's been a sharp rise in threats against journalists in recent years. The verbal abuse was even worse than usual today. . . . Which just reinforces why it's important to call out this dark strain of antimedia sentiment, apart from the attack in Annapolis."

So critics of the press were fueling mass murders? More: Isn't relentless criticism of Donald Trump as a democracy-killing authoritarian endangering *his* safety? We will never know how many death threats investigated by the FBI have resulted from maniacs influenced by the press.

The Stelters on the media scene are not concerned that when a crazed leftist shoots at Republican congressmen during a baseball practice, almost killing House majority whip Steve Scalise, the "awful rhetoric" against Republicans by the left played a role. But it did. The shooter, James Hodgkinson, listed *The Rachel Maddow Show*, *Real Time with Bill Maher*, and the radical left public radio show *Democracy Now* as his favorites. We don't blame the shooting on MSNBC or HBO or Brian Stelter, but it's unquestionable that this anti-Trump and anti-GOP rhetoric is vicious and is fueling rage against him for the far left. They should blather a lot less about press criticism encouraging violence. They should give some serious thought to the reverse.

Trust Us, Our Sources Are Reliable . . .
and Reliably Anti-Trump

One way our "news" media wield power and influence is by hiding the identity of their sources. Doing so allows them to pile the worst dirt on Trump in the worst way. Don't shoot the messenger, they'll say, look at the messenger—the mythical "anonymous" source.

Stories with anonymous sources are routinely trashed by the press if they advance a conservative perspective. Then-deputy White House press secretary Sarah Huckabee Sanders exposed this notable bit of hypocrisy on ABC's *This Week* when the liberal media blasted President Trump for accusing President Obama of wiretapping him. ABC host Martha Raddatz spit at Sanders about a conservative blog's reporting. "Heat Street, they have two sources with links to the counterintelligence community," she fumed. "That's it. Anonymous sources."

You just want to laugh. Sanders was having none of it. "I love how anonymous sources don't count when it's something that's positive in this administration, and against the former one," she shot back. "You guys use anonymous sources every single day. But now that there are new anonymous sources, it doesn't matter."

Bravo! Old media outlets always present their shadowy sources as automatically impeccable, eternally credible, and nonpartisan. That's easier to do when no one knows their names or backgrounds. Indeed, Raddatz bit down on that notion. "Yes, we do" care, Raddatz replied to Sanders. "*The Washington Post* says this morning that, 'senior U.S. officials with knowledge of the wide-ranging federal investigation into Russian interference into the election said there had been no wiretap.'"

As it turned out, this statement was false. Months later, CNN and its anonymous sources reported that former Trump campaign manager Paul Manafort was indeed wiretapped at Trump Tower—and not only was Manafort working out of Trump Tower, he was *living* there. Were those "U.S. officials with knowledge" ignorant? Were they lying? How many of them were there who all said the wrong thing? We'll never know. The *Post* will never tell us.

So why are we all supposed to genuflect to the *Washington Post* and the *New York Times* when they publish breathless stories taking on the White House, relying on their favorite "senior U.S. officials"? Because, as the *Times*'s own media columnist wrote on the front page in 2016, it was critical that the press needed to be "oppositional" and defeat Trump since he was a "demagogue playing to the nation's worst racist and nationalistic tendencies" who "cozies up to anti-American dictators" and "would be dangerous with control of the United States nuclear codes."

And if that includes using "anonymous sources" who don't tell the truth and, as has been documented, sometimes don't even exist—so be it.

There are all manner of allegations that Obama administration holdovers in the intelligence community have tried to take down Trump. Isn't it possible—even probable—that these liberal newspapers are relying on Obama holdovers and granting them all the benefits of anonymity? Isn't it possible that "senior officials" are offering talking points authored by Barack Obama himself? We'll never know.

Liberals get really upset when their critics slam anonymous sources for pushing a secret agenda. In May 2017, CNN was claiming that President Trump was sharing delicate classified information on ISIS with the Russians. National Security Adviser H. R. McMaster roundly denied this. To discuss this further, CNN anchor Kate Bolduan brought in ex-Navy SEAL Carl Higbie, who mocked the sources making these accusations for "hiding" in anonymity.

Bolduan went nuts. "Carl, please! Do not even start with me that you're just going to attack sources! That is ridiculous!" she yelled. Higbie would have none of it and poignantly asked his CNN host if he thought McMaster was lying when he denied the report. Bolduan shouted back, "Do not attack these stellar reporters of CNN who had their sources!" To which Higbie calmly replied, "Tell these stellar reporters at CNN I am going to attack right now, and say 'Guess what? I'm not going to believe them [the sources] because they are staying anonymous. If they stand behind the story, come out, face the cameras.'"

Higbie had nailed it. This entire story was shadowy, to say the least. Classified information that can't be shared with the public is inappropriately disclosed to top Russian officials, but the anonymous sources unveiling this are allowed to do so and must be trusted. The point here isn't just trying to ascertain what happened. It's trying to figure out what happened when we don't know the motives behind those accusing Trump of wrongdoing when everyone seems weaponized one way or the other.

In September 2018, the liberal media's feverish overreliance on anonymous sources to bash Trump reached a new low. The *New York Times* published an entire essay by an anonymous "senior official in the Trump administration" warning that Trump was too reckless to be President. It was bombastically titled "I Am Part of the Resistance Inside the Trump Administration." We were told that the anonymous senior official used an intermediary to get in touch with the *Times*'s editorial page staff. Naturally, they were supremely delighted to cooperate. The writer's identity was allegedly so secret that all the *Times*'s news reporters writing feverish articles on all the repercussions in Washington were kept as blind as bats about who was behind this manufactured spectacle. We were to believe Anonymous Senior Official when he claimed to be conservative, not liberal. We were told by Anonymous Senior Official that other senior officials all over the executive branch "admit their daily disbelief at the commander in chief's comments and actions. Most are working to insulate their operations from his whims. Meetings with him veer off topic and off the rails, he engages in repetitive rants, and his impulsiveness results in half-baked, ill-informed and occasionally reckless decisions that have to be walked back."

In short, "the president continues to act in a manner that is detrimental to the health of our republic."

We were to believe all this explosive "truth" coming from a nameless, faceless source who refused to come forward—and obviously works there!

This was Democratic clickbait: The anonymous op-ed quickly became the most read *Times* article of 2018. The networks had more ammo for their Gatling guns: "Trump isn't mentally fit for office! Not fit for office! Not fit for office!"

It is not surprising in the least that given the fervent *New York Times* animus against Trump, conservatives were deeply skeptical that this anonymous "official" (a) is a truly important official, (b) is an actual conservative, (c) was appointed by Trump, or (d) voted for Trump.

Had a "senior official in the Trump administration" approached the *Times* with an op-ed describing extraordinary achievements by Trump that for national security reasons had to be classified, would the *Times* have run it? They'd have laughed instead.

We won't accuse them of making this writer up. It's obvious that the federal bureaucracy is stuffed with tens of thousands of Obama holdover Trump-hating bureaucrats and thousands that would like to be considered "senior government officials." But the message sounds uncannily like the *New York Times* editorial board or a mind meld with an everyday guest on MSNBC. Anonymous Senior Official sounded like Joe Scarborough's twin. He could be a carbon-copy Comey.

Remember that Jim Comey also used an intermediary to leak his own confidential memos to the *Times* with the hope that the Justice Department would create a special-counsel probe into Trump's interactions with Russia. In both cases, the *Times* was not so much a source of news as an eager conduit for the Resistance.

These media elites insist that they are the sentinels guarding our democracy and as such demand accountability and transparency in government, yet they are exploiting anonymity to send shock waves through the government, and it's somehow antidemocratic to question why they aren't transparent or accountable in their own secret and very ideological manipulations.

Please Don't Remind Anyone the Press Is Unpopular

The alleged truth tellers are addicted to polls, especially when they can use their own polls to push their agenda. When their polls show they've succeeded in driving down a Republican President's approval rating, that is top news, but when their survey shows that a Democratic President has a low approval rating, bad news is no news. They also avoid reporting on polls that show that public opinion of their own profession is in the gutter.

In the first week of Trump's presidency, a Quinnipiac University poll asked point blank, "Do you think that most members of the news media are honest or not?" The media were rated as dishonest, 57 percent to 39 percent. The parties were very divided: Democrats sided with honest 65 percent to 29 percent, and Republicans overwhelmingly distrusted them 86 percent to 13 percent.

Almost two out of three Americans do not trust the news media to tell the truth. How is that not newsworthy?

That result wasn't even mentioned in the Quinnipiac press release. Their headline was "American Voters Say Russia Interfered in Election, Quinnipiac University National Poll Finds; Most Support Sanctions and Many Want More." No network talk show (other than Fox) talked about it. No one editorialized about it. Silence.

Two months into Trump's presidency, a poll by *USA Today* and Suffolk University carried some more eye-opening numbers about public disapproval of the media. They found and reported that President Trump had a 45 percent approval rating, whereas 47 percent disapproved. But they stayed mum about their own numbers. Only 37 percent of Americans approved of their job performance. A whopping 50 percent did not approve.

There have been hundreds of news stories focused on Trump's terrible ratings. Can you name one story acknowledging that the news media reporting those stories are even more unpopular?

There was a massive divide by party identification in this poll. Republican disapproval of the media stood at 78 percent, and only 10 percent approved. The numbers for the Democrats were the reverse: 69 percent approved and 19 percent disapproved.

The pollsters offered another media question: "President Trump has said journalists and the media are the enemy of the American people. Do you agree or disagree?" After the media's relentless attacks on Trump for making this claim, the poll would provide them the evidence that Trump had dishonestly overreached with this most honorable institution.

Indeed, many conservatives would steer clear of the proposition that the press is the "enemy of the people" and stick with Steve Bannon's take that the media elite are the "opposition party" to Trump as a far more comfortable statement. But even so, an astounding 64 percent of Republicans in the *USA Today*-Suffolk poll agreed with Trump on the "enemy" label. (Liberals sided with their major-media buddies, 88 percent to 9 percent.)

These pollsters also asked the public if "President Trump is right when he says the news media is [sic] unfair and biased against him" or "The news media is [sic] right when they say they are appropriately holding the White House accountable."

This result clearly demonstrates that the nation is divided under President Trump. Republicans agreed with Trump 79 percent to 12 percent. Democrats aligned with the media's newfound rush to "accountability" 86 percent to 7 percent.

Both sides know the media are liberal. One side sees this as hostility, the other as comfort.

It was no surprise that these numbers were submerged in USA Today. Their front-page story on the overall poll was headlined "Temperament and Tweets Tripping Up President." Reporter Susan Page began: "President Trump gets high marks for leadership amid growing economic optimism, a new USA Today/Suffolk University Poll finds, but questions about his temperament and tweets have cost him the political boost that a president traditionally gets from that good news."

The poll questions about the media finally made a brief appearance twenty-three paragraphs deep in the story—but without the partisan breakdown. "Meanwhile, Trump's attacks on reporters divide Americans: 42% say he is right when he says the news media are unfair and biased against him; 48% say the news media are right when they say they are appropriately holding the White House accountable." And:

"Are the news media 'the enemy of the American people' as the president has asserted? One-third of Americans, 34%, agree with him. Fifty-nine percent disagree."

The media's rating at 37 percent approval/50 percent disapproval? The evidence that the American people don't trust them to tell the truth? Oh, the irony. They left it out.

This pattern revealed itself again in August 2017, when CNN delighted in reporting the results of a poll question that asked: "How much do you trust the things you hear in official communications from the White House? Do you trust almost all, most of it, just some of it, or nothing at all?"

If a daily viewer of CNN chose anything higher than "nothing," to this question, you'd assume he was a victim of the opioid epidemic. Twenty-four percent chose "almost all" or "most," and 30 percent picked "nothing at all." Forty-three percent picked "some of it," as people tend to reach for the middle option in a poll.

Proving once again its inability to say anything, anything at all positive about this administration, CNN presented these poll results as "only 24 percent trust the White House" and pitched it as a glorious victory for the "objective" media and independent "fact checkers."

On his show *Reliable Sources*, CNN host Brian Stelter turned to Angie Holan of the liberal site PolitiFact. "I admit this is a softball, but does this poll show the strength of journalism?" The liberal reporter agreed that of course it did.

But guess what CNN didn't ask in this poll to test public confidence: "How much do you trust the things you hear from the press? All of it, just some of it, or nothing at all?"

Or even better: How about a CNN poll asking if the public believes *it*?

While we're at it, do you recall CNN ever asking, "How much do you trust the things you hear in official communications from the White House?" during the Obama years?

That said, let us acknowledge that CNN did assemble a "National Report Card," and in addition to grading the politicians, they asked the public to give a grade to themselves. They surely winced at the results: 49 percent gave the media an F, and 19 percent gave them a D. (Just 4 percent awarded them an A.) This, to be sure, also had a partisan breakdown, with most Republicans objecting to the media's thrill-up-their-leg devotion to Obama.

On some occasions, the media are really embarrassed by their poll results. In July 2017, a PBS/NPR/Marist poll asked how much people trusted the Trump administration and then how much they trusted the media. Thirty-seven percent said they had a "good deal" or a "great amount" of trust in Team Trump, and only 30 percent said the same about the media. Ouch!

Yes, give PBS credit for covering its survey. NPR's Tamara Keith lamented that "these numbers are part of a very long trend of institutions losing trust from the American people; and that . . . puts America at risk." This ignores the point that the media have undermined trust in nearly every other institution in America; the media are the last folks who have a right to complain about America being placed at risk.

But don't give them too much applause. When NPR and PBS found a similar hostility to the media in January 2018,

NPR briefly discussed it and its political director Domenico Montanaro used it to denounce the president: "Trump has talked a lot about fake news. . . . It looks like Trump's attacks may be working because 53 percent of Republicans say they have no confidence in the media at all, and that's pretty bad when the truth and fairness, objectivity are the pillars of a free press."

Truth, fairness, and objectivity? Is that what Sarah Huckabee Sanders has been finding in the White House briefing room?

An April 2018 poll by Monmouth University presented an interesting take on how the public views "fake news." They asked respondents, "Do you think some traditional major news sources like TV and newspapers ever report fake news stories, or not?"

A whopping 77 percent of those polled said yes—31 percent said it happens regularly, and 46 percent said it happens occasionally. Only 21 percent said the media did not offer fake news.

The Monmouth pollsters also asked, "Do you think these sources report these stories on purpose in order to push an agenda or do they tend to report them more by accident or because of poor fact checking?" Forty-two percent picked "push an agenda," 26 percent went with "poor fact checking," and 7 percent said "both equally."

Poll questions like this don't specify what kind of fake news is being discussed, but the network evening news shows have aired more than 2,000 evening-news minutes since the inauguration obsessing over the probe into Russian collusion with the Trump campaign, which is still unproven. Is there any doubt that a wide swath of the American people believe that there's a fake-news angle born out of a political agenda?

This question was interesting: "When you use the term fake news, does it only apply to stories where the facts are wrong? Or does it also apply to how news outlets make editorial decisions about what they choose to report?"

Only 25 percent were prepared to give the media a mulligan about incorrect facts; a whopping 65 percent defined it as the way news outlets choose stories, clearly indicting the media as political activists. They choose to exploit a few carefully chosen facts to undermine Trump and the Republicans, and when Republicans object, they are accused of being hostile to "the truth."

President Trump's attacks on the "fake news media" have taken root because they're true, and demonstrably so. It is not democracy that dies in darkness, it is the credibility of the institutions now attempting to undermine it. The *New York Times* had it right. "Truth: It's more important now than ever."

6

Those So-Called Fact Checkers

SAMANTHA GUERRY WANTED GEORGE Stephanopoulos to know that her friend Dr. Christine Blasey Ford was ready to testify. "When she shows up today, she will be completely cooperative and ready to tell her truth." After Ford testified, Senator Cory Booker wanted the world to know he believed the sexual assault accusation against Judge Brett Kavanaugh: "She came forward. She sat here. She told her truth." Republican strategist Suzette Martinez agreed, "I believe that's her truth. And I believe her story. . . . And I could see it on her face," she wrote. But then she threw a screwball. "But I could also see it on Judge Kavanaugh's face that that is his truth."

There's only one problem with these statements. None makes sense. Truth is not relative. Truth just is. Anything else is opinion. Ford had hers, Kavanaugh his. Only one was true.

That's what's so maddening about the left. Everything is relative depending on the subject's whim. It's the calling card of liberalism: tolerant, open-minded, and everything you believe is "your truth." Unless it messes with their truth. That's when their truth ceases to be relative and reverts to fact.

In 1988, Michael Dukakis was broadsided in ads for looking like an idiot driving around in a tank and in other ads for releasing murderers on weekend furloughs. Did Dukakis's actions cost him the election? Not at all. The media elite decided that George H. W. Bush had won because he hornswoggled the electorate with untrue liberal-bashing commercials. In *Time*, they whined, "Bush won by default, and by fouls." So in 1992 they all decided they would be better "fact checkers," especially in rebutting GOP campaign ads.

During the fall campaign, President Bush attacked Bill Clinton as a tax hiker in Arkansas who would do it again if he was elected president. The ABC, CBS, CNN, and NBC patrols all went on full "ad watch" alert to proclaim that Bush was dishonestly attacking Clinton's economic agenda. Cranky CBS reporter Eric Engberg complained, "Feel-bad ads trying to drag down Bill Clinton are regarded as the only hope. In a multi-million-dollar assault, Clinton is being portrayed as a duplicitous blobhead who governs a *Hee Haw* backwater where only the taxes soar." For good measure CBS brought on an "expert" to say the Bush campaign ad making assumptions about Clinton tax hikes was "lying."

Was Team Bush lying? They were making predictions about the future. Candidates can't predict what will happen if the other candidate wins? If the prediction is based on a desire to smear the opponent—say, President Lyndon Johnson's infamous "Daisy" commercial predicting a nuclear war should Barry Goldwater win—it deserves media investigation and condemnation. But the Bushies were claiming that Clinton was a Democrat and Democrats raise taxes. This is like predicting a rooster will crow at dawn. The media wanted to throw the penalty flag at anything "trying to drag down" Democrats. One party was playing dirty, and the other was just telling it like it is.

In the end, the fact checkers were wrong. One year later, President Clinton signed the largest tax increase in American history. No one fact-checked him.

Election after election it's the same. Republicans are dirty, lying louts; Democrats are the noble victims of horrific assaults by dirty, lying lout Republicans. The left's "fact check" machine is so predictably slanted that it should be dismissed.

CNN's Brian Stelter—who turned seven years old in 1992—must have been salivating when he sent around an Election Day e-mail in 2016 prematurely bragging, "This is the year of the fact-checker." He joked that "Trump made fact-checking great again." The message was unmistakably self-congratulatory: *Thank God for us!* Stelter quoted Brooks Jackson, the director emeritus of the site FactCheck.org: "It's really remarkable to see how big news operations have come around to challenging false and deceitful claims directly. It's about time." Translation: *Son of a bitch! We succeeded!* But this wasn't some historic first beach landing for fact checkers. That spin was especially odd, since Jackson was one of the most aggressively pro-Clinton fact checkers in 1992 . . . at Stelter's CNN.

PolitiFact editor Angie Drobnic Holan triumphantly told Stelter, "All of the media has embraced fact-checking because there was a story that really needed it." She was singling out Donald Trump as that story: "[T]he level of inaccuracy is startling." It was true. Donald Trump's mistakes and braggadocio on the stump gave fact checkers plenty to evaluate.

What about Hillary Clinton? She has to be one of the most duplicitous presidential candidates in history—really, does anyone want to challenge us on that statement?—yet in the eyes of the elites, she's the Mother Teresa of political honesty.

Former *New York Times* executive editor Jill Abramson went so far as to write a newspaper column titled "This May Shock You: Hillary Clinton Is Fundamentally Honest." What evidence would she cite for such a preposterous assertion? She pointed to the fact that "PolitiFact, a Pulitzer prize-winning fact-checking organization, gives Clinton the best truth-telling record of any of the 2016 presidential candidates. She beats Sanders and Kasich and crushes Cruz and Trump, who has the biggest 'Pants on Fire' rating and has told whoppers about basic economics that are embarrassing for anyone aiming to be president."

This was not opinion and not even "her truth." It was "fact," determined by PolitiFact.

From the Reagan years to today, conservatives have been dismissed by the elites as ignorant chumps. Thirty years after Dukakis lost 40 states, nothing's changed, and it's precisely this long-standing ideological arrogance—that conservatives are both intellectually challenged and the most resistant to what "objective" journalists define as reality—that informs the fact checkers.

Here's another fact: A vast swath of the American public believes these grand fact checkers are full of crap. According to a Rasmussen poll during the 2016 campaign, just 29 percent of likely voters trusted media fact checking of the candidates and a whopping 62 percent believed the media "skew the facts to help candidates they support."

Don't you just love the American people? They awarded one big, fat Pants on Fire to the entire national news media. If Stelter & Co. were salivating on election night, they were foaming at the mouth the next morning when it was confirmed that all their efforts had been for naught. In response to liberal outrage, the social-media companies promised to do more to warn their customers of malicious Internet lies by turning to the "independent fact checkers" that a majority of Americans didn't trust to be fair.

Snopes Lecturing the Dopes

When you proclaim yourself a fact-checking website dedicated to helping people you believe are easily hornswoggled, be careful what you wish for.

Snopes.com was one of the earliest sites to check facts, founded in 1994 by David and Barbara Mikkelson to document urban legends and call out hoaxes. For some reason, they felt the urgent need to warn the unwashed rabble about the Christian satire site The Babylon Bee, apparently unable to comprehend that some "fake news" is fake because . . . it's satire. Here's the story Snopes felt a responsibility to debunk: "CNN Purchases Industrial-Sized Washing Machine to Spin News Before Publication." We're not kidding.

"In order to aid the news station in preparing stories for consumption," the story began, "popular news media organization CNN purchased an industrial-sized washing machine to help its journalists and news anchors spin the news before publication."

Now, who really believes you put news stories in a washing machine? The fact checker at Snopes, that's who. Snopes felt the urgent need to call this out as "FALSE." Dear reader, we promise we aren't making this up. Their humor-deprived headline was "Did CNN Purchase an Industrial-Sized Washing Machine to Spin News?" The subhead: "The news media organization reportedly invested in mechanical assistance to help their journalists and news anchors spin the news before publication."

Snopes co-founder David Mikkelson claimed he had found people dumb enough to take The Babylon Bee piece literally and enough of them to warrant his expert analysis. "Although it should have been obvious that The Babylon Bee piece was just a spoof of the ongoing political brouhaha over alleged news media 'bias' and 'fake news,' some readers missed that aspect of the article and interpreted it literally."

Guess what happened next? Because Facebook uses Snopes as one of its fake-news-flagging sites, The Babylon Bee's owner, Adam Ford, received a little note that an "independent fact checker" found "disputed" information in his group's humor. Facebook warned Ford, "Repeat offenders will see their distribution reduced and their ability to monetize and advertise removed." Ford found this message outrageous enough to post it on Twitter.

After Ford called out the social network, Facebook apologized in a statement. "There's a difference between false news and satire," it assured the world. "This was a mistake and should not have been rated false in our system. It's since been corrected and won't count against the domain in any way." Snopes did not apologize and correct.

There was another tidbit left out of this story by Facebook (and obviously Snopes). Facebook had monetized Snopes, giving them $100,000 in 2017 for being part of their fact-checking partnership. There was probably nothing in the agreement calling on Snopes to show a grain of responsibility for its own misstatements. Left-wing fact checking means never having to say you're sorry.

The Babylon Bee had a field day with all this, responding with spoofs titled "Snopes Launches New Website to Fact-Check Snopes Fact Checks" and "Facebook Sends Warm Reminder to Publishers That It Is in Complete Control of Their Livelihood." Something tells us the merry band at The Babylon Bee is not finished with their overseers.

We found out for ourselves how Snopes tilts to the left during the 2016 campaign. After national media outlets made a big deal out of racist David Duke endorsing Donald Trump, conservative journalist and Trump supporter Jeffrey Lord posted a blog on NewsBusters pointing out that the same reporters hadn't noted that the Communist Party USA was urging a vote for Hillary.

Mayday! Mayday! The Snopes headline harrumphed: "Did the Communist Party of the USA Endorse Hillary Clinton?"

They decried Lord's NewsBusters article as "FALSE," claiming that "CPUSA did issue a statement urging members to vote against Trump, even if they didn't particularly care for Clinton. The group did not, however, formally endorse Clinton, Sanders, or any other candidate in the 8 November 2016 presidential election."

What did CPUSA publish? Read the lengthy statement for yourself on its website, dated October 30, 2016. It declared its unequivocal position on the election at an international address in Hanoi (where else?).

The statement praised Bernie Sanders and his socialist programs, underscoring that he needed to run as a Democrat as a matter of *realpolitik*. Sanders was saluted for moving his newfound party even farther to the left and praised for pressing his socialist agenda on minimum wage increases, free college tuition, clean energy, and a massive infrastructure investment. CPUSA made it clear where all this exciting socialist-endorsed-by-communists energy could be found: "Organized labor, Black and Latino organizations and progressive movements are in support of the platform and are working for the election of Hillary Clinton."

And her opponent? "Trump represents the most extreme positions within the [Republican] party. His base is composed of open racists, such as David Duke a leader of the Ku Klux Klan, who has said Trump is 'rehabilitating' Hitler's image and other xenophobic, homophobic and misogynistic elements." It goes on and on.

Hillary Clinton needed to be elected and Trump defeated, but it's "FALSE" to say the Communist Party was implying that its backers should vote for Hillary as the best strategy . . . because it wasn't "formal." Snopes even went to the CPUSA, which dutifully issued a statement denying that it made any endorsement. (Communists never lie to advance their goals.)

It gets better still.

Try being an actual finder of fact and tell us how the following is not an endorsement. On the *People's Daily World* website, CPUSA Chairman John Bachtell disagreed with a radical-left "safe state" strategy to vote for Clinton in the battleground states but vote for Jill Stein of the Green Party in the solidly blue (safe) or solidly red states.

"This is a flawed strategy. First, like it or not, we have a two-party system. One of the two major parties will win and govern. If this were a parliamentary democracy different tactics would be called for," Bachtell argued. "Many leaders of labor, civil rights and other democratic grassroots movements, including democratic socialists, are leaders within the Democratic Party. To call for a vote against Clinton is to separate oneself from this electoral coalition."

Which college-educated fact checker could not deduce that this was a statement insisting that all the radicals needed to vote for Hillary? Any fact checker this dumb might believe that you put news stories in washing machines.

PolitiFact or PolitiFlacks?

The most blatantly biased fact checker is PolitiFact, which began as a project of the liberal newspaper the *St. Petersburg*

Times (later the *Tampa Bay Times*). It's now a project of the nonprofit Poynter Institute (which also owns the newspaper). PolitiFact has been sustained by large grants from liberal foundations that include the Ford Foundation, the Bill and Melinda Gates Foundation, and the leftist Craig Newmark Foundation. (Newmark is the founder of Craigslist.)

PolitiFact founding editor Bill Adair admitted that this fact-checking gig was awfully subjective. When a supportive interviewer suggested that their measurements contained some personal opinion, Adair admitted, "Yeah, we're human. We're making subjective decisions. Lord knows the decision about a Truth-O-Meter rating is entirely subjective. As Angie Holan, the editor of PolitiFact, often says, the Truth-O-Meter is not a scientific instrument."

And there you have it: one truthful statement coming out of PolitiFact. But to acknowledge that truth demolishes the idea of PolitiFact as an impartial judge, so the left simply rejects that . . . fact.

You really didn't need Adair to confirm the obvious, however. Back in 2013, long before Trump ran for president, the Center for Media and Public Affairs at George Mason University detected a serious tilt on the Truth-O-Meter.

In a four-month study period, CMPA found that PolitiFact rated 32 percent of Republican claims as "false" or "Pants on Fire," compared with 11 percent of Democratic claims—a 3 to 1 margin. Conversely, Politifact rated 22 percent of Democratic claims as "entirely true" compared with 11 percent of Republican claims—a 2 to 1 margin.

A majority of Democratic statements (54 percent) were rated as mostly or entirely true, compared with only 18 percent of Republican statements. By contrast, a majority of Republican statements (52 percent) were rated as mostly or entirely false, compared with just 24 percent of Democratic arguments.

Do we detect a trend?

Liberals can argue that they shouldn't have to observe some quota in which everyone is equally truthful and should be able to call balls and strikes as they see them. But there is an overwhelming, ongoing pattern of tagging the right-wingers as cheaters on these websites. The umpires have it rigged.

The default position for the media elite is to rate liberal politicians "True" and conservatives of every faction "False." During the 2016 campaign, this liberal-favoring pattern continued at PolitiFact. Among Republican presidential contenders, Ted Cruz landed on the "false" side of the Truth-O-Meter 65 percent of the time, and Rick Santorum 55 percent of the time. Newt Gingrich, who actively supported Trump, was fraudulent 57 percent of the time, too. But what about Democrats? President Obama was ruled false 25 percent of the time, and Bernie Sanders only 30 percent of the time. This is the guy who routinely makes crazy socialist statements such as "the business model of Wall Street is fraud."

It's not just the quality of the fact checking but the quantity. Ted Cruz and Elizabeth Warren were both elected to the Senate in 2012. Cruz was assessed for truth on 114 occasions by PolitiFact through 2016, but Warren? Only 4, and not a single False or Pants on Fire. And for the record, PolitiFact never evaluated Warren on the Truth-O-Meter when she claimed to be part Cherokee Indian.

Overall, they rated Donald Trump as Mostly False/False/ Pants on Fire 77 percent of the time during the primary campaign. Conversely, they rated Hillary Clinton on the wrong side of the facts 27 percent of the time. PolitiFact awarded its Pants on Fire tag to Trump fifty-seven times to Hillary's seven. From September 1 to Election Day, conservatives and Republicans were scolded as Pants on Fire twenty-eight times (fully fourteen of those tags were for Trump). Liberals and Democrats? Only four (and only one for Mrs. Clinton). That's a 7 to 1 tilt, and an obscene 14 to 1 tilt for the presidential candidates.

This anti-Trump pattern continued in 2017 and 2018. Donald Trump was the dominant target, with 297 evaluations, and of those, 205 (about 69 percent) were Mostly False— or worse. Democratic leaders in Congress, by contrast, drew dramatically less attention. Senate leader Charles Schumer drew just nine evaluations (three on the True side, four on the False side, two Half Trues), and House leader Nancy Pelosi had twelve (five on the True side, six on the False side, one Half True). Trump had more Pants on Fire ratings (thirty-three) than all the ratings of Pelosi and Schumer combined.

Overall, in 2017 and through November 2018, conservatives and Republicans were tagged as Pants on Fire liars in ninety-eight articles. Liberals and Democrats? Fifteen. That's a margin of more than 6 to 1.

In September 2017, PolitiFact demonstrated its cozy feelings for Hillary Clinton when Hillary's book *What Happened* came out. They decided to fact-check the book and couldn't find anything inside it they could describe as "False." *Not a thing.* That includes blaming the news media for her loss (they were 91 percent anti-Trump). They played cute with Hillary's claim that hot sauce boosts the immune system with sort of a verbal wink. "Take it with a grain of salt. . . . We don't think the link to hot sauce per se has been peer-reviewed."

PolitiFact's Jon Greenberg was delighted that Hillary quoted Jill Abramson calling her "fundamentally honest," using PolitiFact. Mrs. Clinton underlined that they "found I told the truth more than any other presidential candidate," whereas Trump was "the most dishonest candidate ever measured."

Greenberg happily remembered, "We fact-checked Clinton 196 times from the moment she announced her candidacy in the spring of 2015 through Election Day 2016. Of those 196 fact-checks, 100 rated True or Mostly True. That means 51 percent of Clinton claims we fact-checked were basically accurate. Of candidates we fact-checked at least 50 times, only one did better: Sen. Bernie Sanders. . . . Clinton, however, does better if you only count True statements that we rated."

Only a blind Democrat can't see a pro-Democrat bias here.

We would suggest that PolitiFact should have fact-checked Hillary's book on page 366: "For years, Fox News has been the most powerful and prominent platform for the right-wing war on truth. [Roger] Ailes, a former advisor to Richard Nixon, built Fox by demonizing and delegitimizing mainstream media that tried to adhere to traditional standards of objectivity and accuracy."

PolitiFact's 2017 "Lie of the Year" was a Pants on Fire ruling from May 12. Trump was slammed—surprise! But for what? It was a typically vague/garbled/confusing Trumpian declaration to NBC anchor Lester Holt: "This Russia thing with Trump and Russia is a made-up story. It's an excuse by the Democrats for having lost an election that they should've won." A listener would hear that "Russia thing with Trump and Russia" as a reference to collusion with the Russians to steal the election away from the Democrats. Further, the charge that Russia had helped Trump steal the election was one of Hillary's endless list of excuses. And not one shred of evidence had been uncovered by his Democratic enemies (that includes the press) to buttress the charge. And every Democrat in America, along with most Republicans, believes she blew the election.

So Trump was not just right, he was completely right. Guess where PolitiFact went?

PolitiFact massaged that phrase into their Lie of the Year as "Russian election interference is a 'made-up story.'" PolitiFact editor Angie Drobnic Holan said, "A mountain of evidence points to a single fact: Russia meddled in the U.S. presidential election of 2016. . . . After all this, one man keeps saying it didn't even happen. When the nation's commander in chief refuses to acknowledge a threat to U.S. democracy, it makes it all the more difficult to address the problem. For this reason, we name Trump's claim that the Russia interference is a hoax as our Lie of the Year for 2017."

"This Russia thing with Trump and Russia is a made-up story." Trump wasn't denying that the Russians meddled. He was denying they meddled *working with him*.

Unsurprisingly, Holan added: "Readers of PolitiFact also chose the claim as the year's most significant falsehood by an overwhelming margin." The mostly liberal "readers of PolitiFact" underline one reason why the firm's targeting is so tilted: they provide a lot of tips that help PolitiFact choose which statements they evaluate and "correct."

One of the most embarrassing fact-check articles on PolitiFact in 2018 explored this urgent national concern: "Does Mike Pence call his wife 'Mother'?" PolitiFact devoted an entire article to whether the vice president has called Karen Pence "Mother" around the dinner table.

PolitiFact's John Kruzel explained: "The old-fashioned quality of Vice President Mike Pence's relationship with wife Karen has made their marriage something of an obsession." But to whom? "We decided to break from our usual mission of analyzing the nitty gritty of public policy to look into this unusual feature of Pence's relationship that has captured readers' interest." In other words, their own.

What exactly is unusual about calling a wife "Mother" anyway? Kruzel obviously doesn't. We don't either. So? Hundreds of thousands do or have done so.

Kruzel was inspired by an article in *Rolling Stone*—yes, a fact checker turned to a magazine notorious for a fake story about campus rape. "We found several people willing to go on the record that Pence calls his wife 'Mother,' but we were unable to find video or other documentary evidence, so the claim will remain unrated." In fact, a Pence spokesman had called the claim false, but who cares? Yet that's all they had. So if you can't prove something is factual, why write about it? Aren't the fact checkers just spreading an unverified tale, silly clickbait for bizarre Pence haters?

Well, yes. But "Mother" wasn't enough. This deeply religious Christian couple needed to be attacked viciously. PolitiFact quoted several liberal Democrats insisting that "he called his wife f—ing Mother!" but couldn't PolitiFact find someone who wasn't a Democrat? Kruzel interviewed a reporter who could only recall it. "Offhand, I'm going to say that I did hear him use that term on at least one occasion, but it's not a clear memory," said Jim Shella, a political reporter with Indianapolis-based WISH-TV Channel 8. "It certainly fits with his general demeanor."

This article was unverified gossip about something absolutely unremarkable—hardly something PolitiFact should be proud to publish. But they were pleased. It was an attack on a conservative.

The *Washington Post* Aha Squad

The *Washington Post* "Fact Checker" project run by former State Department correspondent Glenn Kessler is best known for piling up an impressive-sounding anti-Trump number. On January 21, 2019, the *Post* announced that Trump had uttered 8,158 "false or misleading" claims in the first two years of the Trump presidency.

Let's face it: Trump has a history of controversial statements. Sometimes they're vague and confusing. Sometimes it's hyperbole. Sometimes they're misleading. And sometimes, yes, he lies.

But 8,158?

To characterize their findings, they pointed to a single day, in September 2018, "In that single day, he publicly made 125 false or misleading statements—in a period of time that totaled only about 120 minutes. It was a new single-day high. The day before, the president made 74 false or misleading claims, many at a campaign rally in Montana. . . . Trump's tsunami of untruths helped push the count in the Fact Checker's database past 5,000 on the 601st day of his presidency. That's an average of 8.3 Trumpian claims a day, but in the past nine days—since our last update—the president has averaged 32 claims a day."

It would be utterly pointless to try to compare their animus against Trump to that of any other politician they might supposedly be checking. There is one great white whale being hunted, and that ship has sailed.

Some of these "misleading" statements read like uncharitable liberal nitpicking. On September 11, 2018, the President tweeted "Small Business Optimism Soars to Highest Level Ever | Breitbart." The *Post* then just suggests that poll is worthless. "Trump is citing a survey by the National Federation of Independent Business, a conservative group. The group's small business optimism index broke a 35-year record in August. The survey was mailed to a sample of 5,000 members or small businesses, and from that pool, the NFIB got 680 'usable responses.' The response rate was a relatively low 13 percent and it's not clear that this survey gives a full picture of small business optimism."

So the NFIB, arguably the most respected small business association in America, took a poll and found that small businesses are optimistic about the future.

But Trump had no right to say so.

What more "full picture" do you need? There is a seemingly endless parade of polling data confirming small business optimism since Trump took office. Only "Look at me!" "Look at me!" Barack Obama would deny this reality. This fact.

Think of that argument and then know that in Liberal Land, the 5,001 number is translated as "5,001 false statements" or "5,001 lies," and the liberals tweet: "This must be a record for how many times a president has lied."

The *Post* liberals are especially unhappy when Trump repeats an "error" again and again, sometimes because of his penchant for exaggeration. So they report that among his most repeated clunkers (seventy-ninety times) is "African-American unemployment is at the best number in the history of our country," when black unemployment has been measured only since 1972.

But their most repeated "lie" (at 225 times) is Trump claiming "Russian 'collusion' was just an excuse by the Democrats for having lost the Election." Now that Mueller's report is out, we see that, there is zero evidence that it cost the Democrats the election, yet how many times have they said otherwise? If Trump was technically wrong about the black employment rate, he was now officially right about Democrats' excuses.

No matter. Wrong and wrong.

The *Post* and other fact checkers leaped on a March 18, 2018, tweet by President Trump: "Why does the Mueller team have 13 hardened Democrats, some big Crooked Hillary supporters, and Zero Republicans? Another Dem recently added . . . does anyone think this is fair? And yet, there is NO COLLUSION!"

Kessler demonstrated how fact checkers have an irritating habit of verifying Trump's facts and then mercilessly mangling them with "context" to undo those facts. Kessler argued: "Mueller is a registered Republican, as is Rosenstein, who appointed him. Publicly available voter registration information shows that 13 of the 17 members of Mueller's team have previously registered as Democrats, while four had no affiliation or their affiliation could not be found, the *Washington Post* reported. Nine of the 17 made political donations to Democrats, their contributions totaling more than $57,000. The majority came from one person, who also contributed to Republicans. Six donated to Clinton."

So Kessler confirmed that the Mueller team has 13 Democrats, some big Hillary supporters and donors, zero Republicans, and zero Trump donors. Moreover, Rosenstein isn't on the "team"—he appointed Mueller. Trump had tweeted "the Mueller team."

Let's reverse the process and guess how the *Post* would have interpreted it. If a "registered Democrat" had been named special counsel to investigate Hillary and signed up thirteen Republicans and no known Democrats and of those nine, six had made big contributions to the GOP and none to Democrats, how do you suppose the *Post* would have reacted had Hillary declared this to be a pro-Republican cabal? There would have been no fact checking. The *Post* would be too busy running editorials slamming the investigation.

Then Kessler got cute. "It's worth noting that Trump was big donor to Democrats, including seven times to Hillary Clinton, before he decided to run for the Republican presidential nomination" and was a "registered Democrat" during the George W. Bush years.

Meaning that perhaps this Mueller army of Democratic lawyers and donors might have become Republican in time for the investigation. And we are meant to take these fact checkers seriously?

The next argument was even more dreadfully lame. "Federal regulations prohibit the Justice Department from considering the political affiliation or political contributions of career appointees, including those appointed to the special counsel's office," Kessler reminded his readers. "So Mueller is legally prohibited from considering the political affiliations of the people he has hired." Working for a year or two for a special investigation simply does not match the title "career appointee," and the idea that Mueller is "legally prohibited" from considering party affiliation is a complete nonstarter. Mueller hired a pile of D.C.-law-firm buddies and associates whose politics he knew intimately. Inside Washington, this argument can't be made with a straight face.

Kessler uses a Pinocchio system for rating lies. Getting "two Pinocchios" isn't so bad, but try saying that to anyone who gets that award. "Four Pinocchios" is the Pants on Fire rating. During the campaign, Kessler reported, "Trump earned significantly more four-Pinocchio ratings than Clinton—59 to 7. . . . The numbers don't lie."

Of course they do.

They never showed a similar aggression when Barack Obama unloaded his whoppers. How about when Obama proclaimed at a closed-door session in Boston, "We didn't have a scandal that embarrassed us." Forget "Fast & Furious," Benghazi, and all of its attendant and astonishing lies, the millions of taxpayer dollars that disappeared at Solyndra, the IRS smothering Tea Party groups, the Clinton Foundation's pay-to-play shakedown north of hundreds of millions of dollars, or the Uranium One sale to Russia. We could go on and on. The liberal "fact checkers" like Kessler routinely ignored all of that. Obama got away with a bold-faced lie—because he knew they'd never call him out. Kessler's self-impressed slogan is "The Truth Behind the Rhetoric." It doesn't get better than that. Actually, it does. On the *Post*'s "About the

Fact Checker" page, they boast of Kessler's praise from other liberals: "Kessler has long specialized in digging beyond the conventional wisdom, such as when he earned a 'laurel' from the *Columbia Journalism Review* for obtaining Federal Aviation Administration records that showed that then-President Bill Clinton had not delayed any scheduled flights when he had a controversial haircut on an airport tarmac." Digging a Democrat out of a politically embarrassing gaffe—getting a $200 haircut on an airport tarmac—that's where the elites earn their wings.

Kessler demonstrated his desire for liberal approval by appearing on the Comedy Central show *The Opposition with Jordan Klepper*, a failed knockoff of *The Colbert Report*. Right off the bat the question arises: Why in the world is a supposedly impartial and allegedly serious political fact checker going on a left-wing, anticonservative, anti-Trump comedy show? Like Stephen Colbert, Klepper played the character of an idiotic conservative to please a liberal audience. Kessler proclaimed, "In terms of fact checking, Hillary Clinton is like playing chess with a real pro. Fact checking Donald Trump is like playing checkers [laughter] with someone that's not very good at it. It's pretty boring." Klepper shot back: "You find Donald Trump boring." Kessler said, "Yes! His facts are so easily disproven, there's no joy in the hunt."

That's an apt metaphor. Trump is the prey, whereas Hillary Clinton is a chess-playing pro. After he made this comparison, Klepper asked, "Why should we trust you?" to which Kessler replied, "I'm completely dispassionate politically. I just look at the facts."

7

The Snowflakes in Tinseltown

HOLLYWOOD MAY NOT HAVE bear-hugged Trump as one of their own when he came to town, but it didn't take long for them to make him one. This man turned his show *The Apprentice* into an immediate smash while establishing himself as an instant pop culture sensation. They saw his business acumen, and so it was a very smart thing for those elites to be seen with him and—snap!—have their pictures taken and then have those photos circulated around town in the hope that the trade mags would pick them up for their high-society pictorials. To seal the deal, they awarded him his own star on the Walk of Fame.

But then Donald Trump started making noises about running for President, as a Republican no less, and Hollywood went berserk.

In the world of politics, a newcomer challenging the status quo typically must overcome three stages of opposition. Stage 1: The Shun. The subject is ignored in the hope that without the oxygen of publicity he'll die at birth. Should he survive, he'll enter Stage 2: The Ridicule. The goal here is to mock the subject ceaselessly until he's reduced to disposable political waste. If the subject still has not been dispatched, the big guns are pulled out in Stage 3: Scorched Earth. Now it's all business—brutal and personal if necessary. The opposition will open up with guns blazing, including, if necessary, firing at the target from behind, until he is useful only to the buzzards. But should the candidate survive, the opposition has no choice but to enter into the final stage: Acceptance.

Those are the rules for the typical newcomer, but Trump was no such thing. Stage 1 never existed because he was already there as an established celebrity; Stage 4 would never exist because they will never stop attempting to kill him.

The ridicule began immediately. In fact, it started years before. In 2011, NBC's Seth Meyers joked at the White House Correspondents Dinner—with Trump in attendance—that "Donald Trump has been saying he will run for president as a Republican, which is surprising because I just assumed he was running as a joke." Journalists burst out laughing; they agreed.

In 2013, from his sidekick perch on *The Daily Show*, John Oliver egged on the idea of a Trump campaign: "Do it. Look at me. Do it! I will personally write you a campaign check now on behalf of this country, which does not want you to be president, but which badly wants you to run!" More audience laughter.

Trump announced his candidacy on June 16, 2015, and you could hear the roars of laughter from his former colleagues.

Meyers took a cheap shot at Trump in August 2015 by comparing him to the former Subway spokesman who confessed to possessing child pornography and paying to have sex with minors. After raising Trump's accusation about fellow Republican Jeb Bush "being out of touch on women's health issues," this late-night comedian quipped in response that the claim was "kind of like Jared Fogle telling you you're creepy."

In October 2015, Stephen Colbert predicted: "Mr. Trump, to answer your call for political honesty, I just want to say: You're not going to be president. It's been fun. It's been great. . . . But come on, come on, buddy! . . . There is zero chance we'll be seeing you being sworn in on the Capitol steps with your hand on a giant golden Bible!" He doubled down with a visual, a photoshopped image of Trump being sworn in at the Capitol, surrounded by actor Gary Busey and rock stars Meat Loaf, Gene Simmons, and Bret Michaels. His audience erupted.

Colbert wasn't alone here. When asked for comments about Trump in March 2016, Rosie O'Donnell proclaimed, "He will never be president!" In May, George Clooney announced: "There's not going to be a President Donald Trump. It's not going to happen. Fear is not going to be something that drives our country."

Even the celebrity in chief, President Obama, got into the act in all his arrogance. He was asked in January by NBC's Matt Lauer whether he could imagine President Trump offering a State of the Union address, and he joked, "I can imagine it in a *Saturday Night (Live)* skit."

The primaries gave way to the general campaign, and though Trump had dispatched no fewer than sixteen opponents, the Hollywood elites still saw him as a joke and the mocking continued, albeit now with an edge. It was getting serious.

The vitriol grew over the summer as Tinseltown rushed to circle the wagons around Hillary. HBO host Bill Maher tweeted his hatred of Trump's sons Donald Jr. and Eric: "Trump's sons look like the date rapist in every after-school special ever."

During the convention, Maher trashed the Republican convention delegates as "this noxious gathering of short-bus lynch-mob people" and asked leftists, "Are you Bernie people voting for Hillary now?" Maher cracked: "This convention did answer a few important questions for the American people, like 'Could another Nazi Germany happen here?'"

Comedian Aziz Ansari was granted space in the *New York Times* to explain "Why Trump Makes Me Scared for My Family." He began by recalling that he told his mother, "Don't go anywhere near a mosque. . . . Do all your prayer at home, okay?" He then announced, "I am the son of Muslim immigrants. As I sent that text, in the aftermath of the horrible attack in Orlando, Fla., I realized how awful it was to tell an American citizen to be careful about how she worshiped."

But gazillions of dollars in campaign contributions coupled with nonstop red carpet fawning interviews was just not enough. She wasn't putting him away. They needed to go nuclear against the man who might, just might pull off the impossible. They had to kill him.

On Colbert's show, Sean Penn summed up the general election philosophically. "Either you can decide to divorce yourself from loving your children and piss on a tree and show that you have the power to piss on a tree," he mused, "or you can go out and vote in a very big way [as opposed to voting in a small way?] for someone like Hillary Clinton, who then you can challenge and support, which is the only way that any kind of president can have any success—and you stick it out for four years.

"Or we can just masturbate our way into Hell."

Just before the election, on *Jimmy Kimmel Live!*, Obama came to read mean tweets about himself, one of which said: "President Obama will go down as perhaps the worst president in the history of the United States. Exclamation point! [signed] @realDonaldTrump." He had a funny rejoinder: "Well, @realDonaldTrump, at least I will go down as a president."

Funny, but as with everyone in the 90210 Zip Code that year, dead wrong.

On Election Day the beautiful people had their balloon popped. Their safe space was gone. The unthinkable was upon them. America not only had jettisoned their candidate, it had rejected *them*. Their bouncy house had deflated. The Obama era was over. You could hear the gearbox grinding. It was about to be put in reverse, and there wasn't a damn thing the beautiful people—so accustomed to getting their way with a public that hung on their every word, no matter how Sean Penn–like idiotic—could do to about it. They'd been crushed by the man they despised. Donald J. Trump was now the forty-fifth President of the United States of America.

On election night they'd fallen apart.

Alec Baldwin's acidulous *Saturday Night Live* Trump impression failed to persuade people, so he tweeted: "The billionaire Republican businessman is close to winning the race and world markets are crashing. He's all yours, America. He's all yours."

Nashville actress Connie Britton spoke for her fellow snowflakes, seeing imminent persecution of all minorities: "Dear Muslim, Mexican, immigrant, refugee, handicapped, black, gay, female human beings, & also dear Earth . . . you are not forgotten. Promise."

The tweets arrived in an avalanche as celebrities tripped over themselves in a mad rush for attention.

Former child star Alyssa Milano asked: "Is it possible that this country is more sexist than racist? May God help us all."

Movie director Joss Wheedon tweeted "Trump cannot CANNOT be allowed a term in office. It's not about 2018. It's about RIGHT NOW . . . Letting Trump take office means burying democracy. Letting him take it without the popular vote means burying it alive."

Or consider the scabrous sex columnist/MTV personality Dan Savage. "Colorado approves assisted suicide," he tweeted. "That's going to come in handy."

Actor John Cusack is a reliable source of spittle: "The fascism is real—what U see is what U get—will be no comforting illusions left to hide in . . . look at it with clear steely eyes."

Or try this one by *Saturday Night Live* cast member Taran Killam on Twitter: "Rural = so stupid."

Chris Evans plays Captain America in the movies and was considering moving to another planet: "This is an embarrassing night for America. We've let a hatemonger lead our great nation. We've let a bully set our course. I'm devastated."

Director Judd Apatow yelled at the Trump voter: "You just elected the swamp! You gave the swamp total control. You are a fool. You didn't do the math. Putin celebrates your ignorance."

Rarely have the elites been more disdainful of and insulting toward the rabble calling itself America.

They kept coming in.

The *West Wing* creator Aaron Sorkin was inconsolable: "Angry young white men who think rap music and Cinco de Mayo are a threat to their way of life (or are the reason for their way of life) have been given cause to celebrate. . . . Hate was given hope."

Scandal actor Josh Malina complained: "Somewhere tonight there's a little, racist, narcissistic, woman-hating, Jew-baiting kid who now knows that he can grow up to be President."

Actor/polemicist Dax Shepard: "Dear all my friends, I was wrong. It wasn't a landslide for Hillary." It could be worse. He could be Lindsay Lohan, who is an embarrassment in so many ways, including her grasp of election laws. "Retweet if you want a recount," she advised.

Finally, in the "What in the Hell Was He Thinking—and Can He?" category, there was this piece of brilliance from comedian Patton Oswalt trying to improve morale with this lesson in American electoral politics: "We survived 8 years of Bush. We can survive 2 1/2 years of Trump."

So who was the Hollywood winner of 2016? My God, it has to hurt. It was the reality-TV star himself, Donald Trump.

NBC had no idea that all along it had been giving rocket fuel to its own political horror show by broadcasting *The Apprentice* and *Celebrity Apprentice* for fourteen seasons.

The Hollywood loser of 2016? There were so many from whom to choose! But we have to give it to Michael Moore. In 2016, Moore's downward spiral continued as his tiresome documentary *Where to Invade Next* (touting socialist wonders of the world) grossed only $3.8 million. But that looked like a bonanza next to *Michael Moore in Trumpland*, his anti-Trump screed released late in the campaign. It grossed less than $150,000.

The January 11, 2017 edition of the *Washington Post* carried a full-page advertisement on page A-5. The top half had large capital letters screaming "NO! IN THE NAME OF HUMANITY, WE REFUSE TO ACCEPT A FASCIST AMERICA!"

"The presidency of Donald Trump is illegitimate," read the ad copy in bold letters. **"By any definition, Donald Trump is a fascist. He has put together a regime who [sic] will carry out this program and worse."**

It even dispensed with the actual voters. **"No election, whether fair or fraudulent, should legitimize this. 'Reaching across the aisle' only legitimizes that which is illegitimate."** This diatribe ran on the very same day that the *Post* hailed Obama's farewell address for identifying "gathering threats to democracy."

Their pompous call to action was meant to read like some form of anti–Declaration of Independence but accomplished nothing more than to underscore the sheer buffoonery of these idiots. "We, the undersigned, know in the depths of our beings, the catastrophe that will befall the people of the world should the Trump/Pence regime assume full power." They blamed it all on that damn Electoral College, which is "an institution set up in 1787 to protect slavery."

The actors who signed this appeal for a coup included Ed Asner, Margaret Cho, Debra Messing, Rosie O'Donnell, David Strathairn, and Michael Shannon. (During the campaign Shannon had cooed, "My mom's a senior citizen. But if you're voting for Trump, it's time for the urn," and for that, *Entertainment Weekly* magazine had praised him as "a patron saint of grumpiness and grief.")

There were plenty more celebrity activists on this list. There were the Hollywood directors Joe Dante and John Landis. There were far-left rebels of music such as the rappers Chuck D and Vic Mensa and the jazz musicians Kurt Elling, Lalah Hathaway, and Arturo O'Farrill. Alternative rockers included Alex Ebert of the band Edward Sharpe and the Magnetic Zeros, Merrill Garbus of tUnE-yArDs, and Thurston Moore of Sonic Youth.

The signatories also include leaders of the Revolutionary Communist Party, which is still committed to that global revolution. It's understandable why they didn't like the elections. This party's constitution rejects democracy itself: "In a world marked by profound class divisions and social inequality, to talk about 'democracy'—without talking about the class nature of that democracy and which class it serves—is meaningless, and worse."

Based on the copy of this ad, it's fair to surmise that the signatories felt very much at home with that sentiment. The Hollywood left is too enriched to ever follow the tenets of communism, but that doesn't mean they can't sound like communists. Pampered multimillionaires of Hollywood, unite! It has a certain ring.

Just as with the press, President Trump would get no honeymoon from Hollywood. The attacks began immediately and continued nightly. There would be no limits in TV comedy when the target was President Donald Trump, and CBS's *The Late Show with Stephen Colbert* proved it. On May 1, 2017, the President cut short an interview with CBS host John Dickerson after an endless barrage of negative questions and mocked his show as "Deface the Nation." Under the rubric of corporate loyalty Colbert returned fire but raised the ante. He called the President a "prick-tator." He then suggested that the only thing the mouth of the President of the United States was good for was as a "holster" for the sexual organ of Russian strongman Vladimir Putin.

All this on national television while his liberal audience both gasped and roared with laughter.

Red-state America had a different reaction. It exploded in anger. Conservatives on Twitter swiftly imagined the reaction had Colbert aimed this "comedic" fire at Obama—not to mention Hillary. It cannot be disputed. He would have been fired before the day was done. Even liberal Democrats knew that this "comedian" had gone too far, way too far.

CBS refused comment to press inquiries. Amazingly, Colbert finally was pressed into a measure of regret . . . by the gay left for disparaging same-sex activity! He bowed to them by slobbering on his show that "anyone who expresses their love for another person, in their own way, is to me, an American hero." Think through the criminal stupidity of that statement.

Does anyone wonder why Trump refused to attend the White House Correspondents Dinner? This is the level of "humor" Trump was expected to endure at the hands of an industry that detests him.

On April 11, 2017, White House Correspondents Association president Jeff Mason of Reuters proclaimed that it would be "unfair" to roast President Trump in absentia—and then hired Hasan Minhaj of *The Daily Show* to roast President Trump in absentia. This man was best known for a savage leftist tirade against Trump during another "objective" TV news dinner, this one for the Radio and Television Correspondents' Association, that included his label for the man: "a racist Cheeto."

Mason's empty promise was surely in response to late-night feminist comedian Samantha Bee, who brought her TBS show to Washington to tape a "Not the Correspondents Dinner" special. In her taping before the dinner, Bee attempted to outdo Minhaj by comparing conservative red-state Skype questioners at the White House to survivalists who drink their own urine and delighted in the smear that Trump paid for Russian prostitutes to urinate on him.

At the WHCA dinner, Minhaj uncorked lame jokes about "Nazi Steve Bannon" and about Education Secretary Betsy DeVos "curating her collection of children's tears" and insisted to the gathered press, "Donald Trump is Liar-in-Chief. And remember, you guys are Public Enemy No. 1. You are his biggest enemy. Journalists, ISIS, normal-length ties. And somehow, you're the bad guys. That's why you guys need to keep your foot on the gas." Or cut off his head.

In a photo shoot leaked in May 2017 by TMZ, far-left comedian Kathy Griffin posed with a bloodied fake severed head of President Donald Trump in the same way ISIS fighters would in videos show the beheading of their prisoners.

How could Griffin think she hadn't crossed a line? In a sense, her ignorance is understandable. Since Donald Trump had been elected, there had been no lines to cross. Anything... everything... has been acceptable. The challenge has been not to temper the outrage but to push its limits.

It was "art," she claimed, normally the effective refuge for scoundrels in that industry who know that their critics would automatically flee rather than entertain the accusation of censorship. But not this time. The public's response was shock, followed by a Mount Vesuvius eruption of outrage.

First Lady Melania Trump lamented: "As a mother, a wife, and a human being, that photo is very disturbing. When you consider some of the atrocities happening in the world today, a photo opportunity like this is simply wrong and makes you wonder about the mental health of the person who did it." Donald Trump Jr. drove home the obvious point: "Disgusting but not surprising. This is the left today. They consider this acceptable. Imagine a conservative did this to Obama as POTUS?"

He wasn't the only presidential offspring offended. "This is vile and wrong. It is never funny to joke about killing the president." That came from Chelsea Clinton.

Despite a videotaped apology, she was dumped by CNN, which had promoted this "comedian" for ten years as New Year's Eve entertainment in Times Square alongside Anderson Cooper.

It tells you everything you need to know about CNN that up to that point, that network had found her antics not just acceptable but admirable. It had first put her on the air in 2007 after an award-accepting rant at the Emmys telling Jesus Christ to "suck it." She'd cracked, "A lot of people come here and thank Jesus for this award. I want you to know that no one had less to do with this award than Jesus."

Griffin always tried to push the envelope during the New Year's broadcasts on CNN. She took off her shirt in 2012 and welcomed 2013 by telling Cooper, "I'm going to tickle your sack," and then she kissed him on the zipper of his pants.

Griffin has long used smears on conservatives and Republicans to boost her career. In 2010, she caused CNN stars John King and Dana Bash to laugh nervously as she described Republican Senator Scott Brown's teenage daughters as "prostitutes." When the predictable complaints arrived, she boasted, "Whenever a statement is issued against me, I'm in heaven. I feel my next special is half-written for me. And then I get to read statements allowed in my live shows which you can go to KathyGriffin.net and see the many, many cities I've picked up for my current tour."

Back then, the gossip site Radar was thrilled to describe Griffin's chat with an unnamed publicist for *Playgirl* magazine: "I asked Kathy what star she'd like to see take a 'celebrity spill' and she said 'I'd like to push Sarah Palin down the stairs.'" She also claimed that Palin became John McCain's running mate by performing oral sex on him. Liberals have coddled this pig for years, and many clearly thought she'd be the toast of the town for her mock beheading stunt. It didn't pan out that way. On CNN, her colleague Jake Tapper denounced the stunt on air, and her sidekick Cooper disavowed it as "disgusting" on Twitter.

The vast majority of Americans were nauseated, but not everyone. The delinquents at the leftist site Vox defended Griffin as "resisting a rapidly shifting world in which women are losing access to basic reproductive health care."

Journalist Molly Ball of *The Atlantic* cynically denounced the Trumps on CNN for objecting to this outrage. "I have a hard time bringing myself to care about something like this. I think it just speaks to the need to see themselves as a victim that they have, that they are constantly being persecuted."

Make no mistake about this: Griffin's assassination theme continued even if she was not the one projecting it. In the summer of 2017, the New York Public Theater put on stage a poorly disguised Trump version of *Julius Caesar* in its annual Shakespeare in the Park production in Central Park. "Caesar" wore a business suit with an overlong necktie and a bushy reddish-blond haircut. His wife, Calpurnia, spoke with a Slovenian accent. It wasn't hard to catch the drift.

The New York Public Theater's website described this revisionist production this way: "Magnetic, populist, irreverent, he seems bent on absolute power. A small band of patriots, devoted to the country's democratic traditions, must decide how to oppose him. Shakespeare's political masterpiece has never felt more contemporary."

Artistic director Oskar Eustis seconded the emotion that Shakespeare's play was "fresh and new" in our modern age of apparent Trump tyranny. "The institutions that we have grown up with, that we have inherited from the struggle of many generations of our ancestors, can be swept away in no time at all."

The central act of the play has Caesar being stabbed to death, but in this modernized version an American flag looms over the bloody carcass of Trumpy Caesar. One audience member, Laura Sheaffer, was shocked. "'They had the full murder scene onstage, and blood was spewing everywhere out of his body," she said. "To be honest, I thought it was shocking and distasteful. I mean it was the on-stage murder of the president of the United States."

This woman's distaste is the left's idea of class in the era of Trump. The LuEsther T. Mertz Charitable Trust (from the Publishers Clearing House magazine-sweepstakes fortune) was the financial patron for all this assassination chic. American Express is the "official card" of this Trump-loathing gang.

It forces us to revisit the obvious: What if Caesar was Obama? Everyone can guess the reaction of the Manhattan-centered national media if this same play had been modernized with a charismatic black president and his fashionable wife with the well-toned arms. From the safe bet department: This scenario would be stillborn in New York City. Consider how the press got a nasty case of the vapors when Rush Limbaugh merely wished Obama's agenda would fail and again when Mitch McConnell suggested that Obama should be denied a second term. Imagine them covering a fictional rendition of his assassination that was meant to entertain.

But a bloody murder of Trump on stage upset no one. The *New Yorker* passed right over it. The *New York Times* couldn't be moved. There were no Starbucks spit takes on *Morning Joe*.

The socialist British newspaper *The Guardian*, last seen taking great umbrage that its reporter was shoved to the floor by a congressional candidate in Montana, described the Trump assassination plot as "taking a somewhat lighter touch with their Trump resistance themes." A lighter touch? Trump being stabbed like a pincushion? How droll!

This time Anderson Cooper offered no tweet that he was disturbed. To the contrary, CNN Sunday host Fareed Zakaria gave it a rave review on Twitter: "If you're in NYC, go see *Julius Caesar*, free in Central Park, brilliantly interpreted for Trump era. A masterpiece." You can just imagine Kathy Griffin shaking her still-attached head in disbelief, wondering how all this could be okay while her severed-head stunt was so controversial. Frankly, we have no explanation to offer.

There's a reason why the numbers for Hollywood award shows are cratering. A wide swath of the audience has grown sick and tired of this arrogant, condescending treatment of conservatives. This industry's brain trust—if one exists—cannot understand that there are probably plenty of liberals also fed up with the endless political sermons coming from an ignorant, self-righteous community that insists that America listen when all it wanted was to watch an awards show.

In September 2017, the Hollywood crowd gave out Emmy awards like candy to *Saturday Night Live* for its sneering satire of Trump's presidential campaign and Hillary Clinton impersonator Kate McKinnon thanked Hillary Clinton for her alleged "grace and grit." Jane Fonda, who will never go away—why won't she go away?—recalled her film *9 to 5*, saying, "Back in 1980, in that movie, we refused to be controlled by a sexist, egotistical, lying, hypocritical bigot." Her co-star Lily Tomlin picked up the attack. "And in 2017, we still refuse to be controlled by a sexist, egotistical, lying, hypocritical bigot." Left unsaid was that in 1980, just as in 2016, their candidate also had the bejeezus knocked out of him.

Picking up the Emmy for best comedy series actor, Donald Glover of the FX series *Atlanta* announced: "I want to thank Trump for making black people Number One on the Most Oppressed List. He's the reason I'm probably up here."

Emmy host Stephen Colbert even compared Trump to Walter White, the murderous drug kingpin at the center of *Breaking Bad*. "I thought you people loved morally compromised antiheroes. You like Walter White. He's just Walter Much Whiter," he joked.

As 2018 began, Oprah Winfrey was welcomed on the stage of the Golden Globe Awards to deliver a sermon.

She drew rave reviews in the press for lauding the press for abandoning its commitment to impartial journalism: "We all know that the press is under siege these days. But we also know that it is the insatiable dedication to uncovering the absolute truth that keeps us from turning a blind eye to corruption and injustice, to tyrants and victims and secrets and lies."

In the new #MeToo era, she had just deftly tied Donald Trump to Harvey Weinstein.

It's noteworthy that it was a *New York Times* report on Weinstein that created the tsunami uncovering sexual harassment in Hollywood. But let's also be blunt here. That so-called insatiable press, demanding that America embrace its commitment to "comfort the afflicted and afflict the comfortable," has been remarkably silent on this sexual-harassment front for decades. Sexual harassment in the 90210 Zip Code is so prevalent that it has its own name: the "casting couch." The press knew about this casting couch, as did everyone. Why did it wait until 2017 to say something? Then Winfrey pulled a rhetorical muscle by telling the victims that "speaking your truth is the most powerful tool we all have." For the love of God. Here we go again with "your truth." It's not a personal truth that Weinstein and many other men abused women with impunity for many years. It *is*. Must *everything* in Hollywood be morally relative?

And speaking of which, where was Oprah all these years speaking that truth of hers?

Winfrey also insisted this sexual harassment is not "just a story affecting the entertainment industry. It's one that transcends any culture, geography, race, religion, politics or workplace." That's slippery, an attempt to distract and diminish. Thespian, heal thyself.

Then the truth came out.

The rapturous reception of Oprah's remarks was followed on social media by old pictures of Oprah kissing Harvey Weinstein . . . just as her fellow Golden Globes preacher Meryl Streep once lovingly described Weinstein as "God."

This industry could not be more hypocritical. Then again, maybe it could.

The same Hollywood moralists tweeting out their #MeToo messages for decades have refused and continue to refuse to budge on the matter of Roman Polanski, who pleaded guilty to raping a thirteen-year-old girl at Jack Nicholson's house in

1977 and skipped out of the country rather than face justice. Where was Hollywood then? Who lectured Polanski at the awards ceremonies?

In fact, in 2003, when Polanski won a best director Oscar for *The Pianist*, his colleagues gave a standing ovation in absentia to this criminal on the lam. Among those standing and clapping was #MeToo moralist Meryl Streep.

It gets better. Six years later Polanski was arrested in Switzerland for his crime, and as usual, a collection of marquee Hollywood names signed petitions of protest. One of the petition circulators was one of the most a powerful men in Hollywood, an iconic producer named Harvey Weinstein.

For many years now, the celebrated thespian Sean Penn has been one of the wackiest activists in the pantheon of the Hollywood left. He made international headlines in January 2016 when he decided he was a journalist and warmly interviewed the murderous drug lord "El Chapo" for *Rolling Stone*, insisting that the poor fellow was "overdemonized" in the war on drugs.

Now Penn no longer thinks he's a journalist but a novelist. Right before the 2016 election, he released an audiobook he titled *Bob Honey Who Just Do Stuff* under the pseudonym "Pappy Pariah." Simon & Schuster was so impressed that it republished it with his own celebrity name attached. As part of the publicity campaign, the corporate synergists at CBS, which owns Simon & Schuster, aired interviews with him on *Sunday Morning* and then *The Late Show with Stephen Colbert*.

What's so intriguing about this book? Among his many talents, this Bob Honey character is an assassin, and he kills elderly welfare recipients for a secret government agency. But guns aren't cool (except when used by El Chapo), so he murders people with a wooden mallet, presumably the weapon of choice for assassins from secret government agencies. In one scene, Honey writes a letter to the president, who is named Mr. Landlord. He wants him killed.

And here we go. "Many wonderful American people in pain and rage elected you. Many Russians did, too," he writes. "Your position is an asterisk accepted as literally as your alternative facts. Though the office will remain real, you never were nor will be. A million women so dwarfed your penis-edency on the streets of Washington and around the world on the day of your piddly inauguration. . . . You are not simply a president of impeachment, you are a man in need of an intervention. We are not simply a people in need of an intervention, we are a nation in need of an assassin. . . . Tweet me bitch, I dare you."

Colbert wasn't in the least fazed by this. He nudged Penn on, asking, "Have the Secret Service contacted you? . . . Because that's the sort of thing you can't make jokes about." (Earth to Colbert: Your company published them.) Colbert wasn't concerned that this popular pop culture figure was publicly projecting the morality of a presidential assassination; he was worried that Penn might get in trouble for doing so. Penn said he wrote the novel as "kind of a venting." It's "venting," just like his fellow actor Jim Carrey was venting by tweeting a drawing of President Trump's two oldest sons being impaled on an elephant's tusks and just like Kathy Griffin vented when she beheaded him. Some venting is encouraged. Other venting gets you fired. It just depends on who is President. Meanwhile, Penn was paid by Simon

& Schuster for writing "literature" that sounds worse than a bad high-school project. The novel's hero is "evading the viscount vogue of Viagratic assaults on virtual vaginas, or worse, falling passively into prosaic pastimes." It appears that Penn has a thing for alliteration on every few pages, as in "There is pride to be had where the prejudicial is practiced with precision in the trenchant triage of tactile terminations." Even the *Huffington Post* quoted this nonsense and warned, "Sean Penn the Novelist Must Be Stopped." They called it a "nausea-inducing mess."

Yet Penn's reputation wasn't diminished in the slightest in Hollywood. In fact, he was saluted. In language he would appreciate, his peers showered kudos on him for his crusade to convert this corrupt con man into constitutional compost.

Impeachment scenarios and 25th Amendment removal fantasies are not just the purview of faux journalists and novelists. They are plot ideas rolling around in the brains of faux television scriptwriters as well.

In February 2017, CBS began pushing its streaming program *The Good Fight*, an even less fictional sequel to the Hillary-inspired drama *The Good Wife*, on its CBS All Access live-streaming channel. This show has the real-life liberal horror of Donald Trump at its center. The liberal lawyer main character, Diane Lockhart, has her firm competing with others to get a piece of the Democratic Party's impeachment business after the midterm elections.

"It's become this wet dream. We wanted to satirize that while [being realistic] about how Democrats, in our imaginations, are preparing to prosecute it," explained the show's creator, Robert King. "With something very controversial in the news, it's always fun to drive toward it, not run away from it." King and his wife and co-creator Michelle promised an episode that exploited the tabloidish DNC-funded Trump-Russia dossier by former British spy Christopher Steele. It debuted in April 2018. It matters not that the dossier is a fake; ends justify the means. The Kings added a little balance in that a liberal character played by Audra McDonald makes it plain that she doesn't care whether the allegations that remove Trump are true or false as long as they work.

The staff at CBS News would approve.

CBS also employed a 25th Amendment plotline over on its cable channel Showtime with its drama series *Homeland*. Here the paranoid female president Elizabeth Keane was fighting with her vice president, who begged her not to create a crisis by firing cabinet members who would vote to remove her. The sexes change, but the premise remains.

On ABC, the show *Designated Survivor* had its noble HUD secretary turned president Tom Kirkman facing a 25th Amendment process after his wife was killed in a car accident and his therapist's tapes discussing the president's mental state were leaked to the press. To be sure, Kirkman is no Trump. He's more of a *Mr. Smith Goes to Washington* character. But impeachment is impeachment. The premise remains.

In the *Washington Post*, TV writer Scott Tobias unloaded an unintentionally funny line that these writers are "working at a time when television has embraced open partisanship, rejecting the firm political neutrality of the past." Both George Bushes and Ronald Reagan—in fact, any conservative in public service—would find that sentence rather curious, don't you think?

Is Hollywood just indulging itself with a liberal fantasy or actively agitating to condition the public to accept impeachment and/or removal of the president as an unavoidable reality? It is both. They swoon at the very thought of Trump's ouster—and believe they can make it happen too. In theory they are right to do so. In recent decades Hollywood has had a bigger political impact—and a far greater cultural impact—than most realize. It conditioned an entire generation to accept the gay lifestyle and completely changed the political dynamics on that issue. It is why issues such as climate change, the right to kill a baby, and the hostility toward God remain viable. But that is accomplished when the industry is disciplined. That is not the case with Trump, however. It is unhinged.

So what is it about our entertainment elites that makes them think they are so much wiser than everyone else? Why do comedians such as Samantha Bee and Trump impersonators such as Alec Baldwin believe they are qualified to pass judgment on anything more than greenroom coffee? They're not just clueless, they're classless.

The arrogance of the late-night "comedians" overflowed in June 2018 when Bee called Ivanka Trump a "feckless cunt." See how Bee's old boss Jon Stewart came rushing to her defense: "You could not find a kinder, smarter, more lovely individual than Samantha Bee. Trust me, if she called someone a cunt . . ." (Translation: Ivanka deserved it.)

Just about anyone with morals this side of Harvey Weinstein would find Bee the personification of repugnance. Not so the entertainment industry. They are the true elites, engorged with self-absorption and disdainful of anyone who misses the point that they are the witty conscience of the country. Standards? They have none. They are above them. Character assassination is good, obscene character assassination even better.

Once again America unexpectedly blew its stack, and once again one of the beautiful people had to take it back. But Bee's arrogance was self-evident in her lame "apology," which began with a sarcastic "Sorry for breaking America." Then she took a shot at her critics, dredging up the tired old saw that comedians are just making comedy.

"Look, if you are worried about the death of civility, don't sweat it," she said. Then it came out, predictably. "I'm a comedian. People who hone their voices in basement bars while yelling back at drunk hecklers are definitely not paragons of civility," she declared. And then she dismissed everyone. "Civility is just nice words. Maybe we should all worry a little bit more about the niceness of our actions." So it was our fault after all.

"Don't sweat it, I'm a comedian" is a get out of jail free card. They can compare conservatives to Hitler, Stalin, Pol Pot, Osama bin Laden, and Satan, but if you think that's too rough, "I'm a comedian." They can pretend to be policy wonks, and when their "facts" crumble, "I'm a comedian." They can make "jokes" about beheading the president, and when the public does not laugh, it's because it doesn't appreciate comedy.

"Entertainers" like Bee should not have a platform to spew hateful, sexist slurs. Just as with Kathy Griffin, there was no sincerity in her apology. Only self-interest. As Bill Donohue of the Catholic League put it, "A comedian has no more right to obscenely insult people than a cop has a right to randomly beat a person up. Neither should be allowed to take cover hiding behind his status."

Liberals have argued that not only did Donald and Ivanka Trump deserve to be "called out" for their inhumanity, every vile insult of his family is somehow Donald Trump's doing. A columnist for the *Washington Post* even held Trump responsible for America's declining birthrate. (Liberals won't bring children into Trump's world, see, and never mind that self-absorbed Hollywood elites would rather abort than bring their children to term no matter who is President.)

What responsibility do they bear for the state of our noxious public discourse today? They put this all on Trump, and surely he shares the responsibility, but it is not he alone, not by a long shot. They were at it long before he hit the political stage. In 2006, Alec Baldwin wrote in the *Huffington Post* that Dick Cheney was a terrorist or "a lying, thieving Oil Whore. Or, a murderer of the U.S. Constitution." In 2010, Jon Stewart welcomed now-infamous sexual harasser Louis C.K. to *The Daily Show* and let him proclaim, "I was going to say that the Pope f---ed boys and I didn't have time." In 2012, Bill Maher welcomed Sarah Palin's vice-presidential candidacy by calling her "a cunt" and a "dumb twat."

Search for any condemnation from their peers.

Or from CNN.

CNN host Van Jones, the former Obama White House aide, interviewed NBC late-night host Seth Meyers with the usual reverence that liberals offer to comedians of the Resistance. "You are doing a phenomenal service to the country," Jones gushed. "You are an icon, a legend!"

Jones asked about the jesters lining up against Trump. "You are really tough on him. A lot of the late night folks are really tough on him," he acknowledged. But then he asked, "Do you feel that the Red State folks have a legitimate complaint when they say all these late night guys are just a, you know, attack squad against the President and there's no diversity there when it comes to ideological diversity or fairness?"

Meyers started with a who-needs-ratings answer sure to displease the bean counters at NBC: "Look. I can understand that they don't like it. And I certainly respect their opinion to choose not to watch." In other words, he'd rather lose his audience than the ability to insult this president in as ugly a fashion as he could envision, far transcending the acceptable norms of comedy, which would be acceptable to conservatives—as they always have been.

Then came the line that makes you reach for a drug test: "With that said, most comedians are pretty consistent in calling out hypocrisy and lying. I don't think, you know, we don't every day just say, hey, we got to attack Donald Trump."

"Most comedians are pretty consistent" on hypocrisy and lying? Does anyone remember comedians hammering Hillary Clinton when she lied or demonstrated hypocrisy as daily moral calisthenics? What we remember is comedians rolling out the red carpet to honor her and women at Comedy Central nearly fainting in her presence as she winked at them.

Then there is Meyers himself, who helpfully lent his star power to the opening of the annual Clinton Global Initiative in 2014. "President Clinton is here! And so is Bill!" The *Washington Post* reported that "Bill grinned and applauded from the audience." Meyers the Merciless really let them have it for their hypocrisy and lying, didn't he?

There's more, of course. In the February 2013 issue of *GQ* magazine, Meyers nominated Hillary for their "100 hottest women of the 21st century." He told them, "I think somebody who is getting sexier every year is Hillary Clinton. Every year she seems better at whatever she's doing."

In April 2015, Meyers took on Peter Schweizer's book *Clinton Cash*, which documents the astonishing corruption of this family. "It's certainly fair to raise questions about the donations to the Clinton Foundation, but it's also fair to be suspicious of the cottage industry of anti-Clinton books that come out every year." Meyers didn't mention his own Clinton Foundation gig from the year before, a conflict of interest if ever there was one. Even George Stephanopoulos could see that one.

These late-night hosts hate Donald Trump so much that the idea that they would make friendly alliances shouldn't be shocking. Nor should it be a surprise that in today's world anything that reflects negatively on this President becomes "news." Thus, when Colbert at CBS called up Jimmy Kimmel at NBC and Conan O'Brien at TBS for a joint mockery of Trump, the liberal media rejoiced.

Vanity Fair called it a "Historic Group Chat," as if these were world leaders engaged in arms negotiations. *Entertainment Weekly* hyped them as superheroes, engaging in an "Avengers-esque collaboration." CNN media reporter Brian Stelter led his *Reliable Sources* newsletter with the headline "Late Night Collusion!"

The "cold open" that Colbert presented on his CBS show was, as usual, a lame series of references to the insults President Trump had issued at a rally in South Carolina where Colbert was called a "lowlife" and Fallon was a "lost soul." Colbert and Fallon greeted each other with these insults.

Colbert and Fallon wrapped up by lamely agreeing to do lunch at the Red Hen, the classless Virginia restaurant that kicked out White House press secretary Sarah Huckabee Sanders and her guests, an act never performed or even contemplated by conservatives toward a Democratic administration spokesperson. Ever.

In 2012, Fallon hosted President Obama for a segment of "Slow Jam the News" in which he let Obama push his agenda and then endorsed it. "Awww yeah. You should listen to the president. Or as I like to call him, the Preezy of the United Steezy." In 2013, Fallon dressed up as a woman and partnered with Michelle Obama for a skit called the "Evolution of Mom Dancing."

But then he committed an offense that negated all that puffery. During the 2016 campaign he interviewed Trump and playfully mussed his hair. After the election he talked to *The Hollywood Reporter* and sounded like a distraught teenager. "Choking up," the magazine reported, Fallon said to his Tinseltown friends, "I heard you. You made me feel bad. So now what? Are you happy? I'm depressed. Do you want to push me more? What do you want me to do? You want me to kill myself?" No, just shut up.

Comedians are expected to do the left's bidding like pop-culture guerrillas. The agitators apparently driving Fallon to brink of suicide threats never minded when Fallon fawned all over Hillary Clinton. But *touch* Trump? Be gone, Satan, be gone!

All is apparently right with the world when leftist talk show hosts salivate over the Democratic leaders. But Republicans can never be normalized or humanized by them. Fallon's hair mussing was treason. The assault must be brutal and personal. The host must insert himself in the political assault. Observation is not enough.

But let's return to CNN's Van Jones and paraphrase his question: Do red-state folks have a legitimate complaint when they maintain uber-blue-state Hollywood has a vicious, arrogant, and thoroughly obnoxious leftist political agenda, embracing as tolerant only that which they tolerate, as enlightened only that which they deem to be so, and as politically acceptable only that which conforms with their perspective on current events?

Yup.

8

The Midterms and Beyond

"IF THEIR AGENDA IS really about just investigations, I think America is too great to have such a small agenda, or vision. . . . The things I hear from Congresswoman Pelosi, it's a lot about investigations. If you listen to [Democratic Rep. Jerry] Nadler sitting on the train, it's all about investigations, right? That's really what their focus has been. . . . They did not win by laying out an agenda, like a pledge to America or a 'Contract with America.' When you talk to them about what they're going to do in January, they think they need to get together to think about their agenda. So the only thing they've talked about is investigating the president, trying to get a tax return and talking about impeachment. Our country is too great for that."

Thus spoke freshly dethroned GOP Majority Leader Kevin McCarthy on CNBC's *Squawk Box* on November 15, dismissing any suggestion of an electoral mandate for the Democrats, who were still taking victory laps a week after recapturing the House of Representatives. The irony was inescapable. The Democrats had no agenda and won. The Republicans had one, then abandoned it and lost.

The betrayals were numerous and infuriating.

The GOP, ostensibly the party of fiscal responsibility, personal freedom, and traditional values, had looked upon Obama's socialist worldview, with its historically reckless spending, its steady transfer of power to the state, and its social policies deliberately undermining America's sovereignty and its Judeo-Christian ethic through unconstitutional government fiat, and declared that—*by God!*—they would put an end to this insanity. In 2010 they were given the House, and the Boehner–Cantor–McCarthy troika proceeded to do . . . nothing. The excuses were endless, the most comfortable being the need to control the Senate, which was a dodge. The House enjoys the power of the purse, and the GOP leadership had politely declined to avail themselves of it. In 2014 the voters gave them the Senate, as requested, and after all that chest-thumping, again they headed for the tall grass.

Promises made, promises broken.

So they were given the Senate, and again the deflections and dishonesty, pledging at every opportunity to enact their promises while having absolutely no intention of doing so. Again the plea for understanding. *We must have the White House!* Again that was false. A united House and Senate could stop every single one of Obama's radical pieces of legislation or legislate stoppage of his secretive, even more radical executive orders but chose not to do so.

By now conservatives were looking elsewhere for leadership and in 2016 elected a populist outsider as the forty-fifth President of the United States.

Now they had it all. Everything Republicans had pledged was now possible. So what had they accomplished leading up to the midterms?

To his credit, Senator Mitch McConnell performed yeoman's work managing the campaigns to place first Judge Neil Gorsuch and later Judge Brett Kavanaugh on the Supreme Court. Where the latter was concerned, the Republicans led by Judiciary Committee Chairman Chuck Grassley were steadfast, courageous, and even justifiably angry in their support for a man who, along with his wife and little girls, was being subjected to one of the most vicious and dishonest character assassination attempts in recorded American history, orchestrated by the far left on and off Capitol Hill and given instant credibility—including breathless live coverage—by the national news media.

What about this signature pledge—to get rid of Obamacare?

The Congress passed legislation that President Trump stated "essentially repealed Obamacare," except that it did no such thing. Throughout 2017 Freedom Caucus Chairman Mark Meadows had worked ceaselessly for just a partial repeal only to have the late Senator John McCain betray his supporters with his thumbs-down grandstanding for the cameras. (And oh, how the press found that gesture heroic!) In December the Republicans, led by Senators Orrin Hatch, Tom Cotton, and Pat Toomey, were able to attach a provision to the tax bill that obliterated the penalty tax on the individual mandate. This was significant, but the mandate stood—and Obamacare continues to be the law of the land.

President Trump also rammed his promised tax cuts through, but not on the order he'd proposed or should have received on his desk for signature. The federal corporate rate had stood at 36 percent (not including an average 4 percent on top of that for state taxes). According to a Tax Foundation review of the top thirty-five economies in the world, the United States, that bastion of free enterprise and limited government, was paying the highest corporate tax rate on Earth. He got Congress to reduce the rate to 21 percent, which, though not the 15 percent candidate Trump had requested, was still a major success and provided instant jet fuel to the national economy.

The personal tax cuts were far less impressive. In shorthand, as summarized by the Tax Foundation, the rates dropped 2 to 4 percent for most. Standard deductions, the child tax credit, and the alternative minimum tax emption were increased, and the individual mandate penalty was scrubbed. However, the personal exemption was eliminated and the deductions for mortgage interest and state and local taxes were limited. Most alarming (and underreported) is the fact that most of these tax deductions will expire on December 31, 2025.

That was pretty much it for serious legislative results.

The promised wall? Virtually all elected Republicans in Congress had pledged to build a security barrier, and candidate Trump had made it the cornerstone of his presidential campaign. Two years into his administration the Congress delivered peanuts. Trump requested $5.7 billion; the Republicans made a deal with Democrats and gave him only $1.375. Trump wanted a real wall—cement—and was given a fence instead. As of this writing, he has declared a national emergency which he believes gives him the authority to draw the balance from other sectors of the federal government.

It wasn't for lack of money. Like the Democrats before them, the Republicans were out of control with their spending sprees. The party of fiscal responsibility had died.

Obama had been roundly condemned by every Republican in sight for his outrageous deficit spending. In eight years he had increased the national debt by an astonishing 87.7 percent, piling an incomprehensible $9.3 trillion onto the shoulders of generations to come.

You need to look at these mind-boggling numbers. From Obama's inaugural in January 2009 to Trump's inaugural in January 2017, according to the U.S. Treasury, the federal debt increased from $10,626,877,048,913.08 (don't you just love the 8 cents at the end, from a federal government that regularly can't account for tens of billions of dollars?) to $19,947,304,555,219.49.

In just eight years Obama came close to matching all deficit spending under all forty-three of his predecessors—combined.

How many tens of thousands of speeches, press releases, campaign commercials, and media appearances had been delivered by Republicans during that period condemning this as financial suicide and the worst expression of federal irresponsibility and incompetency imaginable? How many tens of thousands of times did Republicans pledge to correct this recklessness if given the chance before there were catastrophic consequences?

In 2016 they were given full control of the budgetary process, and under the leadership of that "fiscal hawk" Paul Ryan they proceeded to accomplish nothing, absolutely nothing. In two years they racked up another $1.86 trillion in debt. The Obama budgets projected deficit spending as far as the eye could see. So too did the Republican budgets.

As of November 2018, the national debt stood at $21,802,839,722,859.62.

Even more incredible, the debt continued to soar even after the feds collected $3,328,745,000,000 in just two years—the greatest tax haul in the history of the republic!

Somehow $3.3 trillion wasn't enough to pay the bills.

It is no longer just the Democrats but also the Republicans that are the party of tax and spend. It's a fact many conservatives are still having difficulty accepting.

In May 2017 President Trump unveiled his fiscal 2018 budget proposal. He proposed to eliminate sixty-six wasteful federal programs for a savings of $26.7 billion. It was a paltry percentage (only in Washington, D.C., can "billion" be defined as "paltry"), but these programs were boondoggles, the kind of programs enacted when bureaucrats decide the federal government is a sandbox for their favorite toy projects courtesy of the American taxpayer—which is to say you, and if not you, your progeny. Every single one of these programs deserved a budgetary firing squad.

The Agriculture Department runs something called the McGovern-Dole International Food for Education and Child Nutrition program. It also hosts the Rural Business-Cooperative Service. The Commerce Department is entrusted with the Manufacturing Extension Partnership.

You're paying for the Department of Education to run things such as the International Education and Foreign Language program and something truly existential called Strengthening Institutions. The Energy Department maintains the Advanced Technology Vehicles Manufacturing Loan Program and the Title 17 Innovative Energy Loan Guarantee Program.

At HHS you'll find the Agency for Healthcare Research and Quality. Homeland Security focuses on the Flood Hazard Mapping and Risk Analysis Program (because that's key to homeland security). The Department of Housing and Urban Development hosts the Self-Help Homeownership Opportunity Program Account. The Interior Department is entrusted with the Abandoned Mine Land Grants. The Justice Department runs exactly what you'd expect Eric Holder's Justice Department to run: the State Criminal Alien Assistance program. The Labor Department gets into that act as well with the Migrant and Seasonal Farmworker Training program.

Add to this the slew of useless and thoroughly obnoxious programs, such as the State Department's $1.59 billion Green Climate Fund and the Global Climate Change Initiative, along with USAID's foreign aid and earmarks worth $4.256 billion.

Then there are the expenditures for not just unnecessary but also inappropriate and/or outdated and/or just plain offensive liberal projects such as the U.S. Institute of Peace, the Woodrow Wilson International Center for Scholars, the National Endowment for the Arts, the National Endowment for the Humanities, the Overseas Private Investment Corporation, the Neighborhood Reinvestment Corporation, the Corporation for Public Broadcasting (including PBS and NPR), and . . .

The list goes on and on. There's a simple test to gauge the value of a product: Imagine the market without it. Imagine the world without stupid agencies such as the Northern Border Regional Commission and the Delta Regional Authority and the Denali Commission. Nothing would change other than that thousands of useless federal employees would be forced to land real jobs.

A total of sixty-six abuses of the American taxpayer. This is the very essence of Washington's leftist elites and their signature arrogance. Their elimination was another key element of the Republican Party agenda: *Give us the power and watch what we do!*

How many of these programs were eliminated by the Republican-controlled Congress?

Not one.

"All politics is local" was the strategic advice for Democrats made famous by former Speaker of the House Tip O'Neill. To do otherwise, projecting instead the party's national agenda of unlimited deficit spending, astronomic taxation, unbridled federal regulation, and crippling defense spending cuts, was to commit political suicide. Moreover, in a local-ized bidding war of promised federal handouts, Republicans couldn't hold a candle to them.

For Republicans the opposite was true. Theirs is the mis-sion to sell a national agenda because their vision of a lim-ited government, a vibrant free enterprise system, a strong national defense, and a virtuous society is at the heart of American exceptionalism. It sells, exceptionally.

In the end it's a simple proposition. When Republicans run as Republicans on a national platform, they win. If they go Democrat-Lite with a localized political agenda, they lose.

When Speaker Ryan announced in April that he was tapping out after the elections, it was presumed that his chief lieutenant would succeed him. McCarthy took the political reins in a closed-door meeting with his GOP colleagues and allegedly urged them to localize their campaigns. Ryan was alleged to have done the same.

Tip O'Neill surely was laughing in his grave.

Now it was Republicans committing suicide, but what choice did they have, really? They couldn't run on a national agenda either. They no longer could hide behind promises. They had been in charge of it all and had squandered the opportunity. They had little to show in the way of accomplishments, and their failures were shocking to their base. But that was looking backward. Looking forward it was even worse. The GOP leadership in both houses had no plans whatsoever to do anything of substance should they somehow manage to retain control. No plan to reduce their out of control spending. Or to end Obamacare. Or to stop illegal immigration. Or to stop the funding of Planned Parenthood. Nothing. Zilch. Nada.

There was no national agenda. There *is* no national agenda for the Republican Party in either chamber of Congress. But McCarthy was correct in his interview with CNBC when he stated that the Democrats didn't "win by having a national agenda" either. Their top campaign issue was health care—but meaning what? Their goal is total government control or at the very least a restoration of the individual mandate, but aside from the Bernie Sanders crazies, no Democrat in his/her/questioning/transitioning/other right mind would openly propose such a thing.

Tax increases? An ever higher debt, with the admission yet again that there was no end in sight for deficit spending? Slash defense spending while China, Russia, Iran, and even North Korea lick their chops? Open borders? Abortion on demand for all through Planned Parenthood, with funding expropriated from those who deem this murder? No, like their counterparts they remained silent. Democrats were Republicans, and Republicans were Democrats.

Because there was no real ideological difference between the parties, given that what one advocates the other supports, the election night coverage was lifeless. Most had projected GOP loss of the House and perhaps slight gains in the Senate. Yet there was a palpable hesitation, even unease in media coverage that night. They'd been thoroughly embarrassed in 2016, and they weren't about to repeat that mistake this time. It was all about the numbers and about the phrase du jour:

The blue wave.

Most Democrats chortled that oh, yes, they'd been awarded a mandate to undo all things Trump. They pointed to the number of seats they'd captured—ultimately the number would be forty-one—which was plenty more than they'd needed to wrest control from the Republicans. In fact, it was the most seats they'd won in the last forty years, going back to the post-Watergate tsunami.

Republicans scoffed. Their evidence: In Clinton's first midterm elections his party lost fifty-four seats. In Obama's, the Democrats lost sixty-three seats. For good measure they threw in the fact that thirty-four Republican incumbents did not seek reelection, giving the Democrats a huge campaign advantage. On election night even leading Democratic political strategists such as James Carville agreed that there was no blue wave.

How did the media play it? On election night 2016 they'd giggled like schoolgirls in anticipation of Hillary's presumed victory, only to stammer in stunned disbelief as the numbers turned against them. They'd been humiliated and had proved that their election models are antiquated and unreliable.

This time they were hedging their bets. For a while no one was prepared even to declare that the Democrats would capture the House.

In the early-evening hours, the returns were puzzling some and CNN still had it "too close to call." Commentator Van Jones was despondent, which is a condition to be welcomed with former Marxist-Leninists. "This is heartbreaking. It's heartbreaking. The hope has been that the antibodies would kick in—that this sort of infestation of hatred and division would draw a response from the American people . . . to say 'no more.'

"That does not seem to be happening tonight. It's not a blue wave, it's still a blue war. . . . I think that sense of helplessness that has really fueled a lot of this outrage and outpouring tomorrow from Democrats may still be there tomorrow, even if we have the House."

When AP finally called it for the Democrats, Van Jones was a happy camper once more ("My heart has been restored!"), but it was obvious to most that there would be no blue wave mandate for them.

On *NBC Nightly News*, Lester Holt conceded that "we haven't seen the blue wave and we've seen the Republicans make a strong stand to hold their seats or increase their seats in the Senate."

On MSNBC, Chris Hayes gave this annoying spin to explain Ted Cruz's victory over Beto O'Rourke, the media's darling candidate of 2018, the one they'd done so much to promote, always lovingly, excitedly, anticipating a glorious victory, an upset for the ages. Now that he'd lost, it was as if a win had never been considered. "A Texas Democrat described the math in Texas like being in a prison and trying to get over a wall."

On CBS, anchor Gayle King pouted. "Clearly the President knows something that the rest of us don't, because what we're seeing so far is his strategy is working," she said before the nine o'clock hour, when it looked like there would be no blue wave. "Not talking about the economy, focusing on immigration, and really scaring people. Scaring people. That seems to be working."

Did we mention that she is a "news" anchor?

Not all "experts" saw it that way. Perhaps the most ridiculous news flash came from NPR's "lead editor for politics" and the former deputy political editor for NBC News, Domenico Montanaro. He was positively giggly about the outcome. He titled his analysis "It Was a Big, Blue Wave: Democrats Pick Up Most House Seats in a Generation." (Obama's sixty-three-seat obliteration didn't count since 2010 apparently constituted a past generation.)

There was another reason for the media's overall lack of excitement on election night, and it's one they'll never concede. This was a political victory for the Democrats, but it was an ideological defeat for the left.

On the GOP side only a handful of conservative incumbents lost, and with the exception of Dave Brat, the Cantor Giant Killer, and to a lesser degree Dana Rohrabacher and Rod Blum. None had any major national political traction. The vast majority of Republicans sent packing were the so-called moderates—why is there no such animal as the "liberal Republican"?—who had bucked the administration, incumbents such as Representative Barbara Comstock, who was elected as a conservative only to betray her constituents by voting against the Obamacare repeal while supporting enough left-wing legislation to earn herself a *Conservative Review* 28 percent "F" rating. To put that in its proper perspective, that's a whopping seven points higher than . . . Maxine Waters (which makes Comstock a "moderate" in the eyes of the press).

Liberal Republicans weren't the only losers that night. Virtually every single media darling running on the Democratic side of the aisle and promoted by the media elites was sent to the showers.

It was the consensus that Senator Claire McCaskill of Missouri was in trouble, but throughout the campaign a lot of media love went her way in the hope that it might help her eke it out. Instead she was crushed by the state's attorney general, Josh Hawley. There was no greater socialist politician running than Tallahassee Mayor Andrew Gillum, who challenged conservative Republican Ron DeSantis in the Florida governor's race. He was regularly feted by the press, especially when he petulantly demanded a recount. He lost.

In that state's Senate race it was wash, rinse, and repeat. Incumbent and longtime media champion Bill Nelson squared off against conservative Governor Rick Scott, lost, demanded a recount, then lost again.

Next door, Georgia gubernatorial candidate Stacey Abrams, a true radical, had been loudly endorsed by Hillary Clinton, comedian Will Ferrell, rapper/actor Common, *Black Panther* star Michael B. Jordan, and others. When Oprah Winfrey joined her to knock on doors, that was when the earth shook. Reporters everywhere dropped to their knees in homage. National coverage everywhere. Abrams also lost, and she was truly classless in defeat, refusing to concede in her concession speech.

But there was no greater leftist heartthrob than Texas Senate candidate Beto O'Rourke, not just because a win would put this Prince Charming in the Senate and on the path to the presidency but because a win would mean the end of Ted Cruz, the most despised Republican in the press before Trump came along. Beto. Like Cher, Rush, and Oprah he has generated first name celebrity status, but unlike Cher, Rush, and Oprah, he's done nothing to earn it. But oh, how the left adored their Prince Charming, ponying up a record $70+ million for his campaign. And oh, how the media fluffed his pillows. He lost.

One media darling, Arizona Senate candidate Kyrsten Sinema, won her race, yet even she was a source of sadness on election night when she was actually losing. Blue wave or not, on the whole it was a far less important outcome than so many political consultants suggest because when the dust settles, the only difference between Republicans and

Democrats is their rhetoric. With the few exceptions outlined here, all protestations notwithstanding, on Capitol Hill the legislative agenda of Obama, Harry Reid, and Nancy Pelosi continues.

But that's policy, not politics, and barring some unforeseen national emergency, from here on out politics is going to overshadow everything.

The new House Democratic majority will go berserk with investigations. There is nothing, but nothing they won't waste taxpayer money on to get rid of President Trump.

Representative Jerrold Nadler and his Judiciary Committee have their guns trained on Trump's attorney general, Bill Barr. Representative Richard Neal and his House Ways and Means Committee are after Trump's tax returns. Representative Elijah Cummings and his House Oversight and Government Reform Committee will hone in on Trump's hush money-for-harlots issue. That committee is going to be working overtime because Cummings also plans to see if Trump violated the emoluments clause by accepting payments from foreign dignitaries who stayed at his hotel. Representative John Garamendi's Transportation Committee will investigate the Trump hotel in Washington. They want to go after Jared Kushner for his proximity to intelligence without a proper security clearance while also demanding to know why loudmouth former CIA director John Brennan had his access revoked. They'll want to investigate Trump's war on the media (we're not kidding about that). Amazingly, they even plan to go after the FBI for failing to adequately investigate the sexual harassment charges against Trump's Supreme Court Justice Brett Kavanaugh even though all Christine Blasey

Ford's supposed witnesses denied they'd seen remotely close to improper behavior and Judy Munro-Leighton even admitted inventing her story about rape in the hope that she could derail his appointment.

Have we forgotten anything? Oh, yes. Have we forgotten anything? Oh, yes. Trump's former Interior Secretary Ryan Zinke, whose conduct had raised concerns within both the Administration and Congress, resigned rather than subject himself to Representative Raul Grijalva's House Natural Resources Committee. The House Education and Workforce Committee has a bullseye on Trump's education secretary, Betsy DeVos. Nadler also wants to investigate the Trump administration for not defending Obamacare enough. Cummings—yes, Cummings again—wants to investigate Trump's "zero tolerance policy" for illegal aliens at the border. And then there's Russia, headed by the zaniest Democrat of them all, the perpetually offended Representative Adam Schiff, who will take the lead with the House Intelligence Committee.

All that . . . noise. All that *intentional* noise.

These are not going to be Hillary Clinton Benghazi and Obama IRS scandals in which real crimes were committed and Republicans ran like cowards. It will be the opposite. These are going to be (for the most part anyway, we predict) legal nothingburgers but political hand grenades meant to build a political case against this administration in 2020. As opposed to one-and-done congressional hearings, the Democrats will be relentless.

There's only one thing this crowd wants, and it's what quite possibly will make them levitate if successful—the proposed impeachment and removal of President Trump.

But there's the rank-and-file Democrats. Their leaders are seeing it differently.

It's interesting. In 2018 Republicans ran on the proposition that they needed to remain in the majority to protect Trump from impeachment. Democrats ran on the pledge that they'd take the bastard out. Now that the elections have been settled, another dynamic is at play. In a very real way the Republicans may be hoping Maxine Waters and Co. will launch those impeachment proceedings, whereas seasoned Democrats are praying it won't come to pass.

Now that the Mueller investigation found no serious allegations of felonious behavior, it looks less likely that Democrats will succeed in an impeachment campaign in the House. Even if they are successful, there's no chance he'll be removed in the Senate. In the process it would wake a sleeping giant in the Trump/GOP base that could easily catapult him to reelection. Just ask Bill Clinton about that one.

Smart Democrats (which necessarily excludes Alexandria Ocasio-Cortez) may find themselves stampeding from those (like AOC) who continue to scream for Trump's head. It explains why the response from the Democratic leadership has been muted, even dismissive, on the subject of impeachment.

Nancy Pelosi is no one's political fool. "I have those who want to be for impeachment and for abolishing ICE. Two really winning issues for us, right?" she told her friends at the *New York Times*. But there's a difference between running on these issues and actually meaning it. "I don't think they're the right thing to do." Democratic whip Steny Hoyer agrees. "Now is not the time to consider articles of impeachment," he said back in 2017, and it's a position he has not veered from since. Asked about this on the eve of the elections on the assumption that his party would capture the House, Joe Biden responded, "I hope they don't. I don't think there's a basis for doing that right now."

But listen carefully to these statements. Everyone has a word lurking in the shadows, implicit and obvious. "I don't think it's the right thing to do—*yet.*" "It isn't the time to consider articles of impeachment—*yet.*" "I don't think there's a basis for doing that—*yet.*"

All eyes were on Robert Mueller. Everyone—including us—expected a harsh condemnation of the president. Anyone who has ever been subjected to a federal investigation will tell you that the more time and money the government spends investigating you, in equal proportion must those agents find something—anything—to justify that effort. Two years and almost twenty lawyers and who knows how many millions of taxpayer dollars later, they had to feel enormous pressure to have something terrible to report. But then Mueller closed down his investigation, saying he found no collusion between Trump and Russia, and wouldn't prosecute the president for obstruction of justice. What an absolute disaster for the Never Trumpers, for Hollywood, for Democrats, and the media. It just vanished, the long-expected Best Scenario for Impeachment, the kind that would cause GOP to surrender to the left's most feverish scandal dreams.

The big question is: Why did the media spend two years endlessly speculating that Trump was toast? How could they justify the "reality" that Trump deserved 90-percent negative coverage on a fantasy of Russian collusion when their expected finale never emerged? If they expected America to believe that Mueller's team never leaked to the press, then why were they so cocky about taking him down?

They didn't spend hours wondering: what if Trump was cleared? They took their war on Trump and packaged it and justified it as journalism, riddled with bias and falsehoods, some the product of recklessness, and other deceptions were deliberate, because with the left, the ends will always justify the means. There were no apologies, as if anybody expected that. When Mueller closed up shop, they went right back to their relentless crusade to ruin his presidency. The badly named "mainstream" press cannot be stopped, populated by hundreds who would sacrifice their firstborn to be the next Bob Woodward taking down not Nixon, who was roundly disliked, but Trump, who they despise and who so many spittle-flecked pundits have likened to every source of evil, from Mussolini to Hitler to the Antichrist himself.

The daily tornado of negative press was designed to energize the Democrat base, and demoralize Trump's base. The most sickening effect of liberal bias is how it demoralizes conservatives and saps their confidence. Every victory only comes by negotiating around an attempted tarring and feathering.

Trump is a marketing genius and has far greater political skills than many had anticipated (including us), so he'll know how to keep his base mobilized. Much to his followers' frustration, however, Trump also will inflict great pain on himself along the way. He picks personal Twitter fights constantly and often unnecessarily with people on whom he should not be focused. He exaggerates and fibs when the truth will serve him perfectly well. He blatantly lies when an artful dodge would suffice. He publicly offends friends and foes alike when restraint and quiet diplomacy are expected, then remains silent when presidential action is in order. All of these are failures, and his enemies will pounce like jackals every single time.

All the same, Trump Nation will go to war for him.

Populists, conservatives, and libertarians will unite under his banner. They are hopelessly outgunned in Manhattan with the traditional news media, as defined by broadcast and cable television, newspapers, and news magazines. Liberals also enjoy almost total control in Hollywood with the entertainment community, which will deploy its formidable assets: television and movies, streaming video outlets, music, celebrity magazines—the list of assets seems endless. Now throw in their newest power center, Palo Alto, home to the ever more radicalized social-media giants. Yet even with all these weapons, the leftist media may not have enough, and the repercussions will be dire. If they lose this war, it will mean having their credibility, which is their very lifeblood, destroyed.

Team Trump has formidable assets too. He has Fox News (except for its news reports, which are remarkably balanced, and Shepard Smith, who has always disliked the president), and Fox is king on cable news. Conservatives dominate talk radio; Rush, Hannity, and Levin all have millions of daily listeners. Conservatives and libertarians maintain powerful websites, from the *Drudge Report* to *Breitbart*, the *Daily Caller* to the *Daily Signal*, from the *Conservative Review* to the *National Review*, *NewsBusters* to *Newsmax*, and so many more. Tens of millions read those online publications.

Then there is the most powerful communications vehicle of them all: social media. The far left may own and control this medium, but Trump Nation has a massive footprint that cannot be ignored. It is not just Trump's 50 million Twitter followers but also FLOTUS's 10 million, and if you throw in @DonaldJTrumpJr's 3 million, you have a real family affair. Beyond that it's the millions upon millions more generated by other leading conservative voices in this field, from @PressSec to @KellyannePolls, from @GlennBeck to @MichelleMalkin, from @NewtGingrich to @RealJamesWoods, from @Heritage to @theMRC, and hundreds more. It's Facebook accounts that regularly reach tens of millions, from ForAmerica to FreedomWorks, Tea Party Patriots to Turning Point USA, Franklin Graham to Steven Crowder, and dozens more. It's podcasts from the likes of Ben Shapiro, Andrew Klavan, and PragerU. It's blogs from *The American Conservative*, *Power Line*, and *The Right Scoop*.

Those are just the national enterprises. Every local community has more of the same.

Should the far left, led by a disingenuous national "news" media, attempt to take out this President through a campaign of character assassination, Trump's supporters will not stand by idly. We pray this clash will never occur, for if it comes to that, the consequences will be truly frightening.

However, should the seas part, inviting dignity to rebound in Congress, intelligence to revisit Hollywood, the free market to reappear in social media, and the news media to return to this simple—and noble—endeavor known as journalism, in which real news is reported accurately, fairly, and truthfully, then no matter the outcome, it will be a celebration of democracy.

9

The Russian Obsession

O N JANUARY 15, 2019, the Media Research Center concluded its analysis of all broadcast network coverage of
the Trump presidency in 2018. The number was astounding:
90 percent negative for the entire year. As with the first year of
his presidency, the top story was the conspiracy theory that
Donald Trump had colluded with the Russians to get elected.

This has been the incessant speculation of the press,
repeated thousands of times. It's been one big unsubstantiated
claim endlessly reported as "news." The elites believe—hope—
that if only the American voters had not been molested by
the Russians, President Hillary would be in the White House
bending their arc of history to the left instead of wandering
the woods bumping into trees and asking what happened.

Since she lost the election, Hillary Clinton has been on an endless and quite amusing "it wasn't my fault" speaking tour. We've lost count of the number of excuses she's presented to deflect from what was surely the greatest collapse and greatest upset in presidential campaign history. Between the time we write these words and the time you read them, she'll probably come up with what? Two or three more? Her most consistent excuse is Russia. Russia bought a president.

The media would insist that it's their job to hold politicians accountable for their policy decisions as well as their scandals. They're right, of course, but it's a dangerous proposition, because in this case, the more you explore their concept of accountability, the more their raging hypocrisy becomes apparent.

It is only Republicans that deserve scrutiny, and we'll prove it.

Let's take a brief tour of just some of the ways the Democrats have undermined America's strength and image around the world with foreign policy fiascoes and international controversies. Many will suggest that Obama and the Clintons (especially) are "too big to fail." They simply cannot be held accountable for their scandalous, even illegal behavior. This presupposes that the media have tried to hold them to account and failed. In fact, they've done the opposite.

The Russian "Reset"

Where were today's red-hot Russophobes in the press corps when President Obama and Secretary of State Clinton declared a friendly "reset" with Russia in March 2009? There was no controversy. Quite the opposite. It was applauded as a welcome change from "testy" relations under George W. Bush. NBC's Andrea Mitchell touted Hillary's meeting with her Russian counterpart Sergei Lavrov as the "Sergei and Hillary Show" and concluded her report, "Most striking of all, after last year's contentious campaign, wherever she goes Clinton leaves no doubt she is an emissary for Barack Obama . . . as the Obama team of former rivals sets out to remake American foreign policy."

This was a reference to the Doris Kearns Goodwin history book *Team of Rivals* about Abraham Lincoln. Speaking of Lincoln, there were ongoing references to him and the other president who magnified the power of the state to a degree so many at the time believed was far beyond the realm of the Constitution.

Days after the 2008 election on ABC's *Good Morning America*, co-host Robin Roberts couldn't stop gushing about the Obama cabinet picks: "Some would say it's a team of rivals, a la President Lincoln, or is a better comparison a team of geniuses as FDR did?" George Stephanopoulos unsurprisingly agreed: "We have not seen this kind of combination of star power and brain power and political muscle this early in a cabinet in our lifetimes."

In 2012, President Obama was caught on an open mike promising Russian leader Dmitry Medvedev, "This is my last election. After my election, I have more flexibility." Medvedev replied, "I understand. I will transmit this information to Vladimir [Putin]." The *New York Times* found this stunning exchange worthy of a story . . . on page 14. It was mildly headlined "Microphone Catches a Candid Obama." The networks briefly noted that "Republicans pounced" on the remark, and that was that. There was no collusion. Time to move on.

During the 2012 debates, Obama mocked Mitt Romney as lost in the 1980s for suggesting that Russia was our most serious geopolitical foe "The 1980s are now calling to ask for their foreign policy back," Obama taunted, "because, you know, the Cold War has been over for 20 years."

The press cheered. It was time to find common ground with our former adversaries. Chris Matthews, who now nightly inveighs against Trump as Putin's plaything, denounced Romney as a fool: "What he said about Russia being our number one enemy in the world today. All this old Cold War stuff seems like a suit he borrowed for the occasion. . . . He doesn't know foreign policy."

The Benghazi Attack

On September 11, 2012, radical Islamic terrorists invaded the American consulate in Benghazi, killing U.S. Ambassador Chris Stevens and three other Americans. On the next day, this became a serious scandal . . . for Mitt Romney! He dared to question the President's decision to "offer an apology for America's values" surrounding violence and protests outside other embassies. On the first night of evening-news coverage, the Big Three newscasts pursued an anti-Romney angle for nine and a half minutes. Obama's outrageous new policy? *Twenty-five seconds.*

Five days after the attack, Obama's national security advisor, Susan Rice, made appearances on no fewer than five major Sunday television shows to declare that it was an unfortunate video produced by some Muslim-hating YouTube troublemaker that was the reason for the deadly assault. This was a boldfaced lie advanced to deflect the blame for those deaths from the Obama administration. The media let Obama implausibly blame that YouTube video for two entire weeks even though Hillary Clinton and others were privately calling it a terrorist attack on the very night of the violence! They also spent their energies aggressively attempting to dismiss any suggestion that Rice had deliberately attempted to deceive the American people.

A week later, CBS News political director John Dickerson made a rather surprising admission, stating that Romney needed to press Obama on being soft on terrorism "because he knows the press isn't necessarily going to make that case for him."

Let's stipulate that the Republican-led congressional investigation into Benghazi was one monumental waste of time, an exercise in organizational tomfoolery that would make the Keystone Cops blush. They accomplished absolutely nothing in their endless hearings. Congressman Trey Gowdy even admitted, "I think a lot of people would say I was a loser." We count ourselves among that number.

The media were even worse. They too were entrusted with the responsibility to investigate an international disaster, but they not only refused to get to the bottom of the Obama-Clinton handling of this fatal policy, they ran interference against anyone who might. And they celebrated Hillary while the Republicans headed for the tall grass.

When Clinton testified in January 2013, then-ABC anchor Diane Sawyer oozed: "Last stand. Secretary Hillary Clinton, filled with fiery emotion in her last appearance before Congress. . . . The indignation. And then, the tears in her eyes. . . . It was a valedictory that showed her indignation and emotion as she ends this tenure on the public stage."

On NBC in 2015, former Republican strategist Nicolle Wallace gushed that her testimony had demonstrated to America that she was "incredibly disciplined" and "incredibly tranquil" and a "formidable presidential candidate." Mrs. Clinton could testify for hours and bask in the knowledge that the rave reviews were guaranteed. Hillary was "filled with fiery emotion," then, "the tears in her eyes," offering a "valedictory that showed her indignation and emotion," "Secretary Clinton as some have never seen her before," "combative, charming, disarming, and clearly ready for a fight," "the political pro . . . giving as good as she got," showing "rare public emotion, reflecting the toll Benghazi has taken on her."

The Iran Deal

The same networks that now imply that Trump is a traitor to a foreign dictatorship relentlessly defended President Obama as he played *Let's Make a Deal* with Iran while that country sought to build nuclear weapons. Easing sanctions on Iran in exchange for dubious (at best) promises to curtail building nuclear weapons was not a popular idea in 2015. Obama couldn't make it a treaty, since it wouldn't pass the Senate. When Obama's "executive agreement" with Iran barely survived a veto in the Senate in September 2015, the media celebrated it as a "major victory" for the President that would define his "legacy."

Under Ronald Reagan, the government sold arms to Iran in an attempt to nudge a release of hostages and fund anti-communist rebels in Nicaragua, and the press thought it was a massive scandal, a sequel to Watergate. But when the *Wall Street Journal* reported in August 2016 that $400 million in cash was flown into Tehran on a cargo plane around the same time that American hostages were handed over, the Obama people ridiculously denied that this was "ransom" money. TV should have had a field day—they had video of Team Obama sending large stacks of euros, Swiss francs, and other currencies stacked on wooden pallets in the dead of night, footage that could be replayed day after day. Obama defended himself by citing how sexy the story sounded. It was controversial "maybe because it feels like some spy novel or some crime novel." They yawned in agreement. It was a one-day story.

The same networks that dogged Reagan relentlessly—Dan Rather & Co. shaming the administration for embarrassing America in front of the world, demanding criminal indictments—were limp noodles for Obama. ABC could barely spend a minute on it, even with that stunning imagery. The coverage was so supine that Obama national security aide Ben Rhodes dared to boast in a *New York Times Magazine* article that the Obama White House had created an "echo chamber" in the press on the Iran deal. He was hailed as "the master shaper and retailer of Obama's foreign-policy narratives, at a time when the killer wave of social media has washed away the sand castles of the traditional press."

The Clinton Foundation

In 2015, author Peter Schweizer released *Clinton Cash*. He'd undertaken the investigation into the Clintons that the investigative journalists—you know, the ones who hold people accountable—had refused to touch. He proved that the Clinton Foundation was heavily engaged with Russia, including the bombshell that on one occasion, the former President accepted a half-million-dollar speech fee from the Russians. No one pays that kind of moolah without receiving something in return, and Clinton ain't that good a speaker. Pay to play, anyone?

The most shocking allegations concerned the Russian purchase of Uranium One, a company that controls 20 percent of America's uranium supply. The company routed millions of dollars to the United States designed to benefit the Clinton Foundation during the time Secretary of State Hillary Clinton served on a government body that eventually provided a favorable uranium decision to Moscow. More pay to play.

But here's how NBC's morning host Savannah Guthrie treated Schweizer in her interview: "Before we get into some of the details, let's put it bluntly. Are you hoping that this book and the issues you raise in it torpedo her candidacy?" He denied it, but she ignored him. "A lot of your critics say, 'Look, you are a conservative and that this is a right-wing hit job.' Are you really claiming to be neutral here?" Is there anything funnier than liberal media outlets demanding neutrality?

From April 2015 through 2018, the explosive Clinton–Russia–uranium story drew a grand total of three minutes and thirty-three seconds of coverage. CNN, which has spent hour after hour, day after day, week after week, month after month obsessing over Russian collusion with Trump, could hardly be bothered with Russian nuclear bribery of the Clintons. To put this in perspective, the Big Three networks offered more than forty minutes of outraged coverage of Trump referring to immigrants coming from "shithole" countries during a private meeting with Democrats. That's more than ten times what they devoted to what quite possibly were multiple public-integrity felonies committed by Hillary Rodham Clinton that could have landed her in prison.

The Dossier

In October 2017, the *Washington Post* reported that Hillary Clinton's campaign and the Democratic National Committee hired the law firm Perkins Coie, which hired the opposition research firm Fusion GPS to dig up dirt in Russia on Donald Trump. The firm then retained former British intelligence operative Christopher Steele, who assembled a discredited dossier from his contacts in Russia (complete with salacious rumors of Russian prostitutes urinating on beds for Trump). "Folks involved in funding this lied about it, and with sanctimony, for a year," tweeted *New York Times* reporter Maggie Haberman.

The year of lying drew no added outrage from the press. Evening news coverage of the uncorroborated anti-Trump dossier, including the story of Clinton and the Democrats funding it, amounted to a mere fifteen minutes of airtime on the Big Three networks in 2017 and another eight minutes in 2018 when former FBI director Jim Comey's book came out. The boredom was palpable.

And even that paltry quarter hour in 2017 was tilted toward Hillary! They loaded stories with Democrats downplaying it, balanced by Republicans . . . also downplaying it. CBS reporter Jeff Pegues first aired Hillary spokesman Brian Fallon and then turned to Republican strategist Alex Conant, a CBS News consultant who "worked for Senator Marco Rubio's presidential campaign." Conant explained, "Every competent campaign does opposition research on their opponents because you want to know your opponent's vulnerabilities. I think hiring foreign spies is a rather aggressive tactic, which is not normal, but it is normal to do opposition research."

Then Pegues garbled the whole mess by adding, "Republicans paid Fusion GPS to initiate the research during the primary." He was referring to Rubio even though it was Rubio's backer Paul Singer who paid Fusion GPS for anti-Trump research months before Fusion hired Steele, the "foreign spy." That might explain why Conant was eager to explain the whole thing away.

No independent Republican was invited to address the fact that Team Clinton had attempted to destroy its adversary through the ugliest form of character assassination imaginable. Pegues knew that hiring British spies to dig up Trump dirt was "rather aggressive," including taking this unsubstantiated dossier from Russian operatives and feeding it to the FBI in an attempt to destroy an opponent, but the story ended there.

Amazingly, some "news" outlets continued to use this dirty dossier to spread unsubstantiated rumors. In one five-day period in April 2018, CNN repeated allegations of "pee tapes"—or Trump hiring urinating prostitutes—no fewer than seventy-seven times in a five-day period. That was truly yellow journalism.

Obama's Domestic Spying

There can be no doubt that the Obama administration was actively pulling for Hillary in 2016. Yes, yes, government employees are not allowed to insert themselves into the campaign, but let's face it—they do. But this time it was different. It was the Obama administration fully invested in the mission to elect Hillary using every weapon in the federal government to bring Trump down.

As the 2016 campaign came to an end, the Obama administration energetically used the government to try to find out what Trump campaign officials might be saying to foreigners. It shouldn't surprise anyone that the story didn't really break out until September 2017, when Bret Baier and Catherine Herridge at Fox News reported that "the requests to identify Americans whose names surfaced in foreign intelligence reporting, known as unmasking, exceeded 260 last year" and one lone official with no intelligence responsibilities made "hundreds" of requests for unmasking. A source identified UN Ambassador Samantha Power as that official.

Try to imagine the media reaction in 2008 had the media discovered that the Bush administration was spying on Obama campaign contacts with foreigners in an attempt to destroy his presidential campaign. The words "hell to pay" spill out. You'd hear the media screaming from the rooftops that a criminal investigation was a foregone conclusion if the rule of law was to survive, etc., etc. But the news that Obama administration officials had improperly "unmasked" Trump officials garnered just twenty minutes of evening news coverage, a veritable pittance.

Then came Russia—and Trump.

Nonstop Coverage of Trump and Russia, Russia, Russia

Robert Mueller was commissioned by Deputy Attorney General Rod Rosenstein on May 7, 2017, to investigate charges of Russian involvement in the 2016 presidential campaign, including the explosive suggestion that team Putin had colluded with Team Trump to steal the election from Clinton. As we sent to press, the Mueller report was released. What evidence do we have of collusion?

None.

Fake news stories suggesting otherwise? Endless.

Two years after President Trump was inaugurated, Fox News host Sean Hannity put on a parade of headlines underlining journalistic fakeries and fiascoes inveighing against Trump on the Russia story. Over and over, the errors resulted from a reckless desire to take Trump down. Those were the mistakes. Others were deliberate falsehoods, fakery at its most dishonest. "Look at your screen!" he demanded.

- "*Washington Post* Retracts Story About Russian Hack at U.S. Utility"—Aaron Short, *New York Post,* January 1, 2017.

- "3 CNN Staffers Resign Over Retracted Scaramucci-Russia Story"—Hadas Gold, *Politico,* June 26, 2017.

- "*New York Times* Forced to Heavily Amend Another Supposed K.T. McFarland 'Scoop'"—Becket Adams, *Washington Examiner*, December 5, 2017.

- "Bloomberg Forced to Correct False Trump-Deutsche Bank Subpoena Story"—Tom Blumer, NewsBusters.org, December 6, 2017.

- "You're Wrong: CNN Steps on a Rake with Donald Trump. Jr. Wikileaks Story"—Matt Vespa, Townhall.com, December 8, 2017.

As he kept posting the damning headlines, Hannity declared, "We can go on all night doing this, one right after another after another after another!"

- "Slate Forced to Correct Report of Unverified 'Theory' on James Comey Memos: 'Mea Culpa'"—Brian Flood, FoxNews.com, April 23, 2018.

- "NBC News Issues Major Correction, Michael Cohen Was Not Wiretapped"—Aidan McLaughlin, Mediaite, May 3, 2018.

- "Brian Ross Out at ABC News Months After Botched Report on Donald Trump, Russia Tanked Stock Market"—Brian Flood, FoxNews.com, July 2, 2018.

- "Mic.com Reporter Deletes Tweet Claiming Alleged Russian Spy Was Photographed in the Oval Office with Trump"—Joe Concha, *The Hill*, September 17, 2018.

- "NPR Blatantly Lies About Donald Trump Jr.'s 2017 Senate Testimony"—Mollie Hemingway, *The Federalist*, November 30, 2018.

Hannity warned, "They are blinded by this hatred of Trump. It's every second, minute, hour of every day. And they are held accountable by almost nobody. They just move onto the next line."

- "Michael Cohen Denies Report of Secret Prague Trip: 'Mueller Knows Everything!'"—Rowan Scarborough, *Washington Times*, December 27, 2018.

- "Five Weeks After *The Guardian's* Viral Blockbuster Assange-Manafort Scoop, No Evidence Has Emerged— Just Stonewalling"—Glenn Greenwald, *The Intercept*, January 2, 2019.

- "*New York Times* issues correction to bombshell report on Manafort, Oleg Deripaska"—Samuel Chamberlain, Fox-News.com, January 9, 2019.

Note that with the exception of the story from *The Hill*, not one came from the wrongfully titled "mainstream press." Every American who copped a plea (Michael Cohen, Michael Flynn, Rick Gates, George Papadopoulos), was convicted (Paul Manafort), or was indicted (Roger Stone) has one thing in common: None has been charged with colluding with the Russian government to get Trump elected. Now add the bizarre: Mueller indicted a pile of Russians who will never see the inside of a courtroom.

We told you a minute ago that the networks devoted fifteen minutes to the story that the Steele dossier, which was what launched the Mueller probe, was a fake. Instead they spent 2,202 minutes (36.7 *hours* in 2017) from January 21, 2017, to February 10, 2019 covering the investigation largely on the basis of speculation and falsehoods! Then, when the Senate Intelligence Committee concluded on February 12 that they had found no collusion with Russia? Zero minutes, zero seconds.

Those 36 hours on evening news is just broadcast TV. Since 2016, cable news has obsessed over Trump and Russia night after night. Where MSNBC and (especially) CNN are concerned, often it's all day, too. Once upon a time, journalism was devoted to the who, what, when, where, and why of a real news event. There's been nothing to report on Russian collusion, and so all of these dimensions have been thrown out the window and replaced with a new one. Today, with a twenty-four-hour news hole to fill, all these "journalists," along with their hand-selected guests, prattle on endlessly in "what if?" questions and "if true" speculation. Lost in all the chatter is that zany showstopper called facts.

At the center of the press coverage of Russia has been the most overdone question in the business: "What did he know and when did he know it?" Truth is, they don't know. But that hasn't stopped the media, or their friends in the Obama administration, or their friends in the Clinton campaign. All freely engage in the conversation because that's what they need to keep the "scandal" going.

The Russia-Trump story serves another purpose. From the start, Hillary felt she could use Russia as her first excuse. In their book *Shattered,* Jonathan Allen and Amie Parnes reported that within twenty-four hours of losing, Hillary Clinton was ordering her campaign to argue that the election was hacked by Russia. Hillary wanted to ensure that "all these narratives get spun the right way," one "longtime ally" told Allen and Parnes. Just as in 1998, when reporters leaped to prove that the conservative evildoers somehow forced Bill Clinton into tawdry sex with an intern, thus causing him to lie about it to investigators, they lunged at stories of Russian interference at Hillary's behest, this time to validate Vast Right-Wing Conspiracy 2.0.

By December, the press was eagerly giving oxygen to any protest against Trump as a dubiously elected Russian pawn no matter how fanatical or staged it was. The perpetually (and professionally) aggrieved were taking to the streets, knowing their allies in the media would dutifully cover them and do so with empathy. The *New York Times* breathlessly reported: "In Florida, protesters swarmed the Capitol rotunda, one hoisting a 'Trump Is Too Rusky' sign featuring a hammer and sickle. In Wisconsin's statehouse, a heckler shouted, 'We're all going to go to war and die thanks to you.'"

These insults and smears were somehow a celebration of democracy in action. No one questioned the veracity of those attacks on the election results, never mind the motives of those pushing this narrative. They were too busy promoting them. The *Times* turned to hyperpartisan Adam Jentleson, a top aide to retiring Senate Minority Leader Harry Reid, who warned, "There's not going to be a grace period this time because everybody on our side thinks he's illegitimate and poses a massive threat."

He was correct. There was no grace period. They couldn't afford a grace period. The goal was to convince America that the man headed to the White House was a poseur, and so the assault was relentless. Shortly before the inauguration, the *Times* insisted that "the uneasiness with Mr. Trump has hardly receded in the nearly six weeks since his election." Of course it hadn't! The press was huddling in the trenches with Harry Reid and his aides, magnifying their unease and then marveling at it day after day, show after show, rag after rag, all the while calling it news. They were not about to admit that their loss was caused by a wretched candidate with $768 million worth of incompetence wasted on her campaign. It had to blame it on Russia and its connection to Trump. It remains Russia-Trump to this day.

On Inauguration Day, January 20, 2017, then-*CBS Evening News* anchor Scott Pelley, a "journalist" who clearly despised the new President, greeted him with this love tap: "As Donald Trump begins his presidency, some of his former advisors are being investigated for possible links to Russian officials." Over the next few weeks, Pelley kept up a barrage of insults. He slammed the new commander in chief on January 23 for "a weekend of tweeting tantrums and falsehoods." On February 6, Pelley criticized Trump's "fictitious claims" and "presidential statements divorced from reality." And in March, Pelley scolded that "Mr. Trump has continually stamped rumors with the seal of the President."

It wasn't just the news media, of course. Everyone on the left with a microphone wanted in on the act. Within days of the Justice Department naming Mueller as special counsel—with Deputy Attorney General Rod Rosenstein asking

Mueller to investigate only Trump and not the Clinton camp for criminally colluding with Russians—the unyielding get-Trump spirit of the media was on display on ABC's *The View*. The ladies begged their guest, former Defense Secretary Don Rumsfeld, to declare that Trump's impeachment was inevitable . . . *if* Mueller found anything troubling.

ABC News legal analyst and *View* co-host Sunny Hostin asked: "If it's true, should he be impeached? . . . If his administration colluded with the Russians to win this election, should he be impeached?" Rumsfeld wasn't about to play that game. He retorted that he hadn't seen any proof of collusion. He wasn't going down that rabbit hole. Joy Behar yelled back Hostin's disclaimer. *"If! If! If! If!"* It simply did not matter to Behar & Co. that there wasn't a shred of evidence. The thoroughly hypothetical "if" was enough to warrant a discussion about removing Trump from office.

(We don't recall Behar or anyone else in her camp ever exclaiming that "if Bill Clinton raped Juanita Broaddrick, he should be put in prison for the rest of his life." And in that case, there was one hell of a lot more than a shred of evidence. There was an eminently believable victim who has never been invited on *The View*. In 2016, Joy Behar even called Broaddrick and other Clinton accusers "tramps." The #MeToo movement goes only so far.)

Despite their proclamations that they are the guardians of facts, the liberal elite wanted to fast-forward beyond that silly thing called evidence and project Trump's ruin as inevitable. Sentence first, verdict afterward, then evidence . . . if any. Impeachment was perpetually on their minds and often on their lips. Month after month went by with no proof surfacing of actual Trump campaign collusion with the Russians. It never mattered, but they weren't about to consider the possibility that this wasn't a story or would turn out badly for them.

The same reporters who effortlessly spread the fake news about "scandal-free" Barack Obama in the face of a mountain of evidence of wrongdoing were now dedicating themselves to the opposite, cementing the proposition that Donald Trump was hopelessly scandal-plagued without the need for evidence. The same journalists who shamelessly whacked away at Kenneth Starr as a modern knockoff of the inquisitor Torquemada were presenting Mueller as the incarnation of Eliot Ness. The only thing consistent about the press was its partisanship.

Take a few cover stories at *Time* magazine to give yourself a sense of the media mind-set. In June 2017, they published a gassy cover story titled "The Lie Detector" that compared Mueller to a mythical deity: ""It goes back to the Greeks, who understood that the peril of kings was hubris, and that hubris was an invitation to the avenging goddess called Nemesis. In Robert Mueller, Trump may have found his."

Mueller was a runner-up for their year-end 2017 "Person of the Year." This time he was called "The Enforcer. . . . A prosecutor known for rigor and rectitude goes after the president's men." *Time* writer Massimo Calabresi gushed that "the special counsel has held the country in his thrall [with] rare bipartisan support and a team a veteran cops and prosecutors, he has made news even when he tried not to." *Time* insisted that criticism of Mueller's partisanship and stone-walling "has hurt the President more than the prosecutor. Mueller is a lifelong registered Republican."

This was a ridiculous statement—and they knew it. They were intimately familiar with the fact that there was Democratic partisanship on Mueller's staff, that thirteen of his seventeen lawyers were Democrats, that nine of them donated to Democrats, and that Andrew Weissmann even attended the infamous Hillary Clinton "Victory Party" in 2016. But Mueller was registered as a Republican, and that was all that mattered. The late Senator John McCain was also a registered Republican and despised Trump. Mueller was immune from even the thought that this might be true of him, too.

For a striking contrast, let's examine coverage of another special counsel. This one was investigating a roguish figure, except that this man was guilty, was forced to pay $850,000 to settle a sexual harassment lawsuit, had his Arkansas law license suspended after committing perjury, and was impeached. Let's dig out *Time*'s "Men of the Year" coverage of Bill Clinton and Ken Starr at the end of 1998. *Time* declared as fact that Starr had engaged in a "witch hunt" and "disas-trously" included stark sexual details in the Starr Report. The magazine responded to Clinton's impeachment with moral equivalence. "The more Starr pushed, the more Clinton stalled. And in the end, each drove the other to a kind of madness." *Time* concluded by suggesting that Starr was also an offender, and "like Bill Clinton, he still dreams of being found not guilty."

Trump Tower Topples?

In July 2017, the media exploded over a meeting in June 2016 at Trump Tower between Donald Trump Jr. and Natalia Veselnitskaya, the alleged "Kremlin-backed lawyer" (she wasn't Kremlin-backed) at which Russians promised "dirt" on Hillary Clinton. But before we get into this coverage, let's stop and consider: So bloody what? At one stage or another, there were probably a hundred meetings between Team Hillary and God only knows who, from the candidate on down, discussing dirt on Donald Trump. It's what campaigns *do*. It's also what journalists *do*.

If the evidence showed that this Russian woman was knowingly an agent of the Russian government offering ammunition to tilt the election and if there was any explicit or even implicit quid pro quo on the part of Team Trump to alter Russia policy in a favorable direction, you had a story, and a big one, too. Indictments and impeachment would follow, and deservedly so.

If. But there wasn't a lick of evidence. Trump administration policy toward Russia was tougher than Obama's! Still the "if" justified the endless speculation that Trump was probably a criminal. America would be faced with the nightmare that it had elected a traitor. Every mini-scoop was inflated into the latest contender in the urgent liberal question "Will this finally get Trump impeached and removed?" The media obsession was palpable. The evidence of their fever could be found on your own smartphone.

On the night of July 11, the CNN app was all ablaze with the Trump Junior jeremiads. One after another, the headlines were panicky and tabloidish:

- "Trump's web of Russian ties grows with Miss Universe links."

- "The most troubling parts of Don Jr.'s e-mail exchange with Rob Goldstone."

- "Kaine: Trump Jr. may have committed treason."

- "Trump Jr.s' e-mails undermine what the White House has been saying."

- "Trump Jr.'s latest e-mail explanation to Sean Hannity doesn't make any sense."

- "How much legal trouble is Donald Trump Jr. in?"

- "Trump Jr. releases bombshell email chain."

The *National Enquirer* would be proud of CNN's passion. In the midst of this stream of speculation verging on mindless gossip, down in the fifth spot, was this other piece of news: "Special ops forces among 16 dead in Marine Corps plane crash." Way down at the number eight spot was this: "Earth's sixth mass extinction is more severe than we thought." But Marines dying and alleged mass extinctions are boring and secondary to wild speculation about Russia. The next headline on the CNN phone app was "Tapper to Trump Jr.: Why so many lies?"

There are no longer any guardrails for CNN. Virtually every "news" story is a blatant attack on Trump. How do CNN's colleagues view this abandonment of any semblance of balance? you ask. The *New York Times* mourned in all seriousness that CNN was losing in the ratings race to "the more ideologically driven coverage of Fox News and MSNBC." We kiddeth not.

When Democrats sit in the White House, they have so many liberal "solutions" to advance that their approval ratings cannot be allowed to be soiled by scandals, and so the media ignore them if possible and spin with wild abandon when necessary. For years, President Clinton could count on reporters to keep Kenneth Starr's investigation on the back burner, insisting that Clinton's good works were being infringed on by a hostile prosecutor doing work of questionable public value. In 1997, as Clinton toured the Caribbean, ABC reporter John Donvan announced, "When the President fended off a Whitewater question by saying, 'Look, I'm just down here doing my job,' the Caribbean journalists burst into applause, in part because they had heard enough about Whitewater and wanted to talk more about bananas."

Donald Trump has received the opposite treatment from the very same media outlets. Scandals have always crowded out policy—unless the press insisted that the policy was itself scandalous, in which case it becomes news. When Mueller first whispered that indictments were coming down in October 2017, ABC's David Wright was thrilled. "Call it Russian roulette!" he declared in an overly excited manner. "The first criminal charges imminent in the independent counsel's investigation of Russian meddling in the 2016 election and possible collusion by Trump associates!" George Stephanopoulos, always the partisan, drooled, "Is it someone close to the White House? Is he going straight to the top?"

All that was missing here was "Please! Please!"

On October 30, 2017, Mueller indicted former Trump campaign chairman Paul Manafort. It had nothing to do with the 2016 campaign. It had nothing to do with Trump. It made no difference. They could attach "Manafort" to "Trump." Even better, they could use "indictment" and "Trump" in the same headline.

The media provided massive coverage—often "breaking news"—of Manafort's troubles—unless the real news undermined their narrative, in which case it was deliberately ignored. In May 2018, presiding federal Judge T. S. Ellis III broadsided Mueller's prosecutors in court. The smackdown was epic. "You don't really care about Mr. Manafort! You really care about what information Mr. Manafort can give you to lead you to Mr. Trump and an impeachment, or whatever." He added what was obvious to anyone looking at the evidence impartially: "I don't see what relation this indictment has with anything the special counsel is authorized to investigate. . . . What we don't want in this country is, we don't want anyone with unfettered power."

But the media weren't examining the evidence impartially. They were way past that. The Donald was guilty, facts be damned.

The Ellis bombshell appeared on the front page of the *Washington Post*, as was appropriate. The networks, in contrast, refused to budge. ABC devoted two minutes to it, and that was that. CBS and NBC managed thirty seconds between them. Taxpayer-funded networks tanked. PBS had nothing, and NPR had one question on a Saturday morning newscast. This was a test of the fairness and balance of the Mueller-obsessed networks, and they flunked, and they couldn't care less. The show had to go on.

Then there were Trump Tower revelations that were omitted. To say they were inconvenient to the prosecution of Trump is an understatement. What follows is something we'll wager is unknown by 99 percent of the American people. It turns out that Natalia Veselnitskaya—that Russian lawyer who had met briefly at Trump Tower with Donald Trump Jr.—had dinner with Hillary-funded Fusion GPS co-founder Glenn Simpson on the night before. *And* the night after the Trump Tower meeting! Simpson boldly insisted that he knew nothing about the meeting in between. And if you believe that, you'll also believe that Bill Clinton's a regular Ward Cleaver.

How could that not be the story? The evidence now pointed directly to a trap that had been sprung by Team Hillary. Now you had real intrigue. If it had been seen as a credible accusation that Don Jr. was colluding with the Russians, given the before-and-after with Team Hillary, was there now not the potential that it could have been far more sinister than that—between the Russians and Hillary?

Network coverage of this *real* bombshell? Zero. Zip. Nada. If the networks wanted to obsess over the Trump Tower meeting, why not devote some serious minutes to this revelation with red flags all over it? Because exploring this behavior would unspool months of wildly speculative reporting on the Trump campaign seeking dirt on Hillary Clinton from the Russians to defeat her. The shoe would now be firmly on the other foot. Now the accusation of treason would fly against the former secretary of state who had shown no hesitation to have her foundation shake down foreign governments for millions.

They were never interested in the notion that Hillary Clinton was colluding with Russians to defeat Donald Trump. Destroying Trump has been the imperative from the start. At the center of it all was not Charles Schumer, or Nancy Pelosi, or the Never Trumpers. It was the press.

In schools, they used to teach that journalism was defined as telling the public what happened today, along with who did it, where it happened, how and why. But too often in political coverage, what's already happened is downplayed and even ignored while "news" channels prattle endlessly about what's going to happen next. That's exactly how the media covered the Russia probe, constantly yammering about the heinous crimes Mueller would find, or how Trump might fire Mueller, or the man who appointed him, deputy attorney general Rod Rosenstein. Collusion was a fantasy all along and underscores a terrible reality. For journalists, the facts just do not come first. These self-righteous leftists who marched under the banner of "objective journalism" while advancing the overthrow of a duly elected president did more than just lose their credibility. They committed professional suicide.

Afterword

The Top Ten: Who Hates Trump The Most?

WHO ARE THE BIGGEST Trump bashers in the press? When you consider that his coverage is regularly in the 90 percent negative range, you can conclude that just about everyone in the media qualifies except for conservative periodicals and radio talk shows, Internet and blog sites, and television outlets. Yet even on these platforms you'll find Never Trumper candidates. That includes the inaccurately pigeonholed Fox News (Shepard Smith, call your office).

For quality, it's just as daunting a proposition. How can you distinguish one ranting journalist from the next? The field looks a little like the beginning of the Boston Marathon, with a cast of thousands, all eager to burst to the front of the pack, elbowing aside the competition with that story (true or not, who cares) or, better yet, that sound bite (ditto) that will generate fist pumps and lazy copycatting from leftist agitators everywhere.

Yet amid the rabble there are some real standouts. This list is subjective, of course, but reflects what we believe and what our colleagues have suggested are those whose minds go into spontaneous combustion mode at the mere thought of Donald Trump as their commander in chief. Some of these so-called journalists are so left wing that they could stand on either side of the podium during a Nancy Pelosi–led press conference. It's not just those in the news business. This list begins with those who are meant to entertain with humor but cannot help frothing at the mouth instead.

10. Brian Williams, MSNBC. How does this disgrace still host a nightly show and serve as a "breaking news" anchorman? When he's gone, he'll be remembered for one thing only: lying. That, of course, does not disqualify a person from anchoring a news program at MSNBC, and so there he sits in all his puppy-dog-looking glory, breaking the important news of the day. At that network reporting breaking news means finding something, anything to pin on Trump, no matter how much of a stretch. When Williams isn't Pinocchioing his bona fides, he's busy demonstrating that he's a master of the absurd. His anti-Trump shtick has included the suggestion that the President hates dogs, because, well, because he used dog metaphors to describe his critics. "Does this president really physically not like dogs?" he asked. "We launched an extensive web search that took us at least a few minutes and could only find one photo in all the land of Donald Trump with a dog." He's a deep thinker.

9. Brian Stelter, CNN. Stelter hosts *Reliable Sources,* which is billed as a show analyzing the media. It's not. It's a weekly red alert to warn CNN's viewers that Trump is a dictator who wants to shut down the free press on the road to perdition. The lectures are endless and obnoxious. When he's not attacking the President for lying, he's questioning his state of mind. "Will President Trump deny reality on a daily basis? Will he make up his own false facts and fake stats? What will the consequences be?" In the course of passing judgment on what does and doesn't constitute truth, Stelter sounds like he's about to wet his pants over Trump. He asks journalists, "Is the Trump presidency a criminal presidency?" and "Are we living through a national emergency?" Only on CNN could a man like this be given a show called *Reliable Sources.*

8. Jorge Ramos, Univision. Ramos may not have the name ID or reach of other TV personalities, but from his perch atop this Spanish-language network, he's the best-known Latino "journalist" in the country and the poster boy for waging total war on Trump without the slightest pretense of objectivity. In fact, he openly campaigned against Trump in 2016. Typical of this was a column for *Time* magazine headlined "Judgment Day Is Coming for Those Who Stay Silent on Donald Trump." He insisted that "when it comes to racism, discrimination, corruption, public lies, dictatorships and the violation of human rights, we have to take a stand." But he's

pitched as the Spanish-speaking Walter Cronkite, anchor of
the nightly *Noticiero Univision* and the Sunday show *Al Punto*.
There's a reason candidate Trump refused to allow this fraud
to heckle at his press conferences, denouncing him for "ranting and raving like a madman" and telling him, "Go back to
Univision!"

7. Philip Rucker, *Washington Post.* Rucker is identified as
White House bureau chief during his regular MSNBC appearances, which are a mockery of objective journalism. His front-
page "news" reports regularly read like editorials. Trump's
scandals stink, and so Rucker wrote about his foreign policy: "For Trump, each bold stroke is like a spritz of Febreze
on his narrative of domestic scandal." The most egregious
example came when President Trump attended the funeral
for George H. W. Bush and Rucker mocked him greeting his
predecessors. There's "the president Trump said was illegitimate (Barack Obama); then the first lady he called a profligate spender of taxpayer dollars (Michelle Obama); then the
president he called the worst abuser of women (Bill Clinton);
then the first lady and secretary of state he said should be
in jail (Hillary Clinton); and then the president he said was
the second-worst behind Obama (Jimmy Carter) and his wife,
Rosalynn." He can't wait to be appointed a columnist. He's
doing it now, with a White House press pass.

6. Chris Matthews, MSNBC. No one can quite capture
the careening swings of liberal excess on cable TV quite like
Matthews, who effortlessly lurches from the Obama leg-thrill
ovations to the Trump spit-drooling rages. His metaphors are

regularly as incoherent as he's unhinged. He's compared the Trumps to the Romanovs—the Russian royal family slaughtered by the communists. (Who are the communists in his scenario? Are they going to kill Trump and Melania and the kids?) He's suggested that Trump's grown children—Donald Jr., Ivanka, and Eric—are like Saddam Hussein's murderous sons Uday and Qusay. He's even suggested that perhaps President Trump should kill Jared Kushner: "You know, one good thing Mussolini did was execute his son-in-law."

5. Chris Cuomo, CNN. Can the son of one ultraliberal New York governor and the brother of another one be taken seriously as a nonpartisan journalist? At CNN all things are possible, and so he can qualify for a job as anchor of *Cuomo Prime Time,* but no observer outside of CNN with the IQ of a potato will take this man seriously. Cuomo evinces a strange disconnect with reality. He's claimed to *Rolling Stone,* "You are rarely hearing my opinion on television," yet he bashes Trump and his voters on a daily basis. In one chat with Don Lemon in 2019, he supported a chef who banned people wearing Making America Great Again hats from his restaurant. "I think the more appropriate analogy to say is, if people were wearing shirts that said 'I hate black people,' would he be okay to say 'Don't come into my place with that?'" In 2018, he said Obama was much more popular than Trump because "America at her best by her nature leads with her heart, not her hate." No opinion there.

4. Every late-night talk-show host. Steve Allen and Johnny Carson hosted *The Tonight Show* and both regularly teased politicians on both sides of the political divide, yet neither ever showed his political colors. They were pros. And by God they were funny! Today's late-night comedians are the polar opposite: partisan and angry, but that really doesn't do it justice. They are off-the-rails predictable and boorish with political humor that regularly descends into the potty, the signature of a comedian who isn't funny. They represent and reflect an industry that despises Trump—from Bill Maher comparing the President to a "terrorist," a "dangerous menace," and "drug-resistant super gonorrhea," to Jimmy Kimmel asking a porn star about the President's penis size, to Stephen Colbert calling Trump the "Presi-dunce" and "prick-tator" who "eats human flesh," to Samantha Bee calling the President's daughter a "feckless cunt." Stay classy. They're not journalists, but they have great cultural influence and deserve a slot high on this list.

3. George Stephanopoulos, ABC. George has never stopped toiling in the public relations fields for the Clintons. He's more than a Clintonite; he's a Clintonphile. Not only has he routinely hosted panel discussions at Clinton Global Initiative meetings, he's even donated $75,000 to the Clinton Foundation. Any news enterprise with a lick of integrity would find an itty-bitty conflict of interest at the idea of this Clinton ex-staffer covering the 2016 campaign—hell, *anything* dealing with Hillary! At ABC, however, this qualified him to anchor *This Week*, the network's flagship Sunday news program. Since the campaign it's been more of the same. Every week he seeks to undermine Trump, including hosting an unprecedented hourlong special in 2017 (which was about fifty-five minutes too long) plugging James Comey's book ranting against Trump. To consider the extent of attention given Comey to eviscerate his former boss, compare it with the coverage Stephanopoulos has provided during his entire tenure at ABC, from *Good Morning America* to *This Week*, to Mark Levin and his five number one bestsellers dismantling the left, which necessarily includes George's former bosses. Not one second. Speaking of coverage, it cannot be disputed that the 91 percent negative coverage Trump received during the campaign was unfair. George would agree, but not the way you think. He felt Hillary Clinton was wronged by the press in 2016, that coverage was "too equal" between candidates. "If you point out a wrongdoing on one side, you have to point at a wrongdoing on the other," he explained, "and they automatically become equivalent and that isn't always fair."

2. Joe Scarborough and Mika Brzezinski, MSNBC. If these two were conservatives, they'd generate their own weekly *Saturday Night Live* mockery. The former conservative Republican congressman is "former" in every sense. He's no longer in Congress, he has formally and most publicly quit the GOP, and he's stopped pretending he's on the right. Mika is Mika is Mika: We all await the first memorable thought coming from this woman. Mr. and Mrs. are true ideological chameleons whose colors change effortlessly to blend with their position du jour. At the start of the campaign they were happily hosting and toasting Trump. In November 2015, Joe touted Trump's "gut instinct and strength," and in January 2016, he said the sight of Trump's plane landing in Iowa "was like the Pope had landed with the Middle East peace pact to end 3,000 years of war." But when they said something he didn't like, Trump took a shot at them—and they came unglued. Today they are the perfect launch pad for MSNBC's daily left-wing character assassination campaign against the President, smug in their hypocrisy. Scarborough has claimed that "sources" told him Trump was suffering from the "early stages of dementia" and smeared his supporters as frenzied fascists looking "like a Mussolini rally." He said that Trump's separation of illegally immigrating parents and children was "just like the Nazis" and that this "tyrannical president" had "used Stalinist barbs to attack the free press." Days before the midterm election, the new Mrs. Scarborough lectured, "If you want a slight check on this man and his unrelenting race to the finish here to make sure he can continue destroying this country, you might want to vote all 'D,' even if it's not your party this time around."

1. Jim Acosta, CNN. CNN's Chief White House correspondent, Jim Acosta, is our winner. We suspect Acosta would protest if he wasn't. He would proudly wear the moniker of the face of the Resistance if it was bestowed on him by us, but we won't do that. No man in the world of journalism has made a mockery of his profession quite like this man. He lives to be obnoxious. Not contrarian, mind you, not the probing reporter who plays devil's advocate to force his target to defend his position. There's something admirable about that technique if that's the purpose. Not so Acosta. He lives to heckle. His goal is not to produce headlines of substance but to *be* the headline, much to the delight of his floundering network that will do anything for attention. If it means mangling the facts while he yells at a White House official—like suggesting to presidential aide Stephen Miller that the only foreign nations that speak English are Great Britain and Australia—or flat-out disrupting a press conference, like when he tussled with a White House intern to hold on to the microphone, refusing to obey instructions from the President and cede the floor to his colleagues, Acosta will do it. There was a reason Team Trump took the unprecedented action of publicly revoking his White House credentials. There's just so much annoyance a man can take from a boring clown. CNN sued, and the White House relented. It shouldn't have. Freedom of the press includes the right to open a seat in the press room for a real journalist. Acosta will keep his look-at-me-look-at-me routine going, but we think he's worn out his welcome. He certainly has with Trump's MAGA army, which heckles him everywhere he shows his face, which makes him pout and complain to his CNN snowflakes: "Honestly, it felt like we weren't in America anymore. I don't know how to put it any more plainly than that." Lost on him was the fact that they are exercising their freedom of speech, something arrogant journalists like Acosta believe is a right belonging only to themselves.

Acknowledgments

Putting together a book analyzing the daily output of the national news media content requires a team effort, and the Media Research Center has the best operation in the business. The MRC News Analysis Division is led by Brent Baker, who has steered this ship since the Media Research Center's founding in 1987. Research director Rich Noyes, his deputy Geoffrey Dickens, and his assistant Bill D'Agostino have compiled the systematic numbers—the indisputable evidence—demonstrating how overwhelmingly negative President Trump's coverage has been.

NewsBusters Managing Editor Curtis Houck and Associate Editor Scott Whitlock help keep the MRC's news-monitoring machine running from early in the morning to late at night, including on weekends, and that was especially true during this book-writing process. They, as well as Senior Analyst Kyle Drennen and analysts Kristine Marsh and Nicholas Fondacaro, carefully combed through all kinds of panicked, frenzied "news" stories without somehow losing their minds.

MRC Latino director Ken Oliver keeps track for us of how Spanish-language media have waged war on the conservative movement; his insights on Jorge Ramos, Trump's biggest antagonist in that media sector, have been invaluable.

After all Brent put his assistant through to help him with four drafts and a thousand attendant details, it's a mystery why Melissa Lopez still works for him. Perhaps it's because she knows how grateful he is. Se lo digo de verdad.

Tim thanks his wife Laura, and his children Ben and Abby, and always thanks God for his parents, Jim and Ann Graham.

Brent Bozell thanks his ever-patient bride Norma and expresses his affection for all of his progeny except for the one son who allowed his own children to climb all over their grandfather while he was trying to work on this book.

Finally, we thank all our friends at NBC, CBS, ABC, PBS, MSNBC, CNN, Telemundo, Univision, the *Washington Post*, the *New York Times*, AP, NPR, and . . . the list is endless. We thank all of you. Without your contributions this book would not have been possible.

Index

Simple **Heart Test**

Powered by Newsmaxhealth.com

FACT:

▶ Nearly half of those who die from heart attacks each year never showed prior symptoms of heart disease.

▶ If you suffer cardiac arrest outside of a hospital, you have just a 7% chance of survival.

Don't be caught off guard. Know your risk now.

TAKE THE TEST NOW ...

Renowned cardiologist **Dr. Chauncey Crandall** has partnered with **Newsmaxhealth.com** to create a simple, easy-to-complete, online test that will help you understand your heart attack risk factors. Dr. Crandall is the author of the #1 best-seller *The Simple Heart Cure: The 90-Day Program to Stop and Reverse Heart Disease.*

Take Dr. Crandall's Simple Heart Test — it takes just 2 minutes or less to complete — it could save your life!

Discover your risk now.

- **Where you score on our unique heart disease risk scale**
- Which of your lifestyle habits really protect your heart
- **The true role your height and weight play in heart attack risk**
- Little-known conditions that impact heart health
- **Plus much more!**

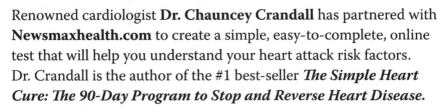

SimpleHeartTest.com/111

PAY ZERO TAXES

Your Personal Guide To The New Tax Law

Trump Tax Cut is your guidebook to the biggest tax cut in history. This breakthrough book reveals hundreds of write offs, tax breaks, credits, legal loopholes, and NEW information that can literally save you a fortune.

Tax Secrets Inside:

- ✓ The **ALL-NEW** change that will instantly help 70% of Americans! Chapter 1 explains how easy it is to cash in.
- ✓ **How you can still deduct the mortgage interest on TWO homes! Tip #12 reveals the details.**
- ✓ Deduct more for medical expenses! The threshold for medical expenses plummets by 25 percent!
- ✓ **ALL NEW! Take $10,000 of distributions from 529s to help cover the cost of home schooling. Tip #184 is a real godsend.**
- ✓ 13 tax no-no's that could trigger an audit. Chapter 12 is a lifesaver.
- ✓ **3 big state-tax deductions most people miss — including tax pros!** The amount you're deducting can easily add up to thousands of dollars. Don't miss TIP #9.
- ✓ Collect rent payments the IRS doesn't count as income. Tip #43
- ✓ **A Better way to save for college. Tip #168 could help millions!**
- ✓ And lots more tax deductions, tips and loopholes!

Claim Your SPECIAL OFFER Now!

Claim your **FREE** copy of *Trump Tax Cut* — **a $19.99 value** — today with this special offer. Just cover $4.95 for shipping & handling.

Get Your FREE Copy

Go Here:
TrumpTaxCut.com/Unmasked